Afghanistan:
The Seeds of Hope

Afghanistan:
The Seeds of Hope

Adjustment of Political Situation,
Strengthening of State Fundamentals and the Problems
of Post-conflict Reconstruction of Afghanistan

Jura Latifov

To order additional copies of this book, contact:
Xlibris Corporation
1-888-795-4274
www.Xlibris.com
Orders@Xlibris.com
47209

Contents

PREFACE

The monograph represented to the view of the reader "Afghanistan: the Seeds of Hope" (Adjustment of Political Situation, Strengthening of State Fundamentals and the Problems of Post-conflict Reconstruction of Afghanistan) seems to be a continuation of the earlier published work by D.L.Latifov "Tajik-Afghan Relations in 1987-1995" (character, contexts). In subsequent years D.L.Latifov analyzes complex processes of the mentioned country which along with its big neighbors China, Russia and Iran exerts a direct influence on geopolitical situation of Central Asia. Dear reader, we hereby represent to you the new book by D.L.Latifov—the author who indicated himself with a number of works dwelling on Afghanistan. Those interested remember his articles of explorative slant: "Hamid Karzai—View from Tajikistan", "On the Issues of Cultural and Spiritual Cooperation between the Republic of Tajikistan and the Islamic Republic of Afghanistan", "The Situation in the Islamic State of Afghanistan and Strategic Goals of Key Players of Anti-terrorist Operation", "Cooperation of Central Asian States with Afghanistan: Myth or Reality?", "Tajik-Afghan Border, Alarm of Nowadays", "Neighbors Being not Chosen" and others published in Mass Media, scientific collections edited both in Tajikistan and abroad.

Now in his new work the author traces the political events in Afghanistan subsequent to September 11, 2001.

The scientist notes that the menace aimed at stability, regional and global security proceeds not so strongly from the inner resistance of military-political forces operating in the country, as due to the factor of expanded influential zones of the Taliban movement which commenced its activities five years ago yet.

In his research the author lays an emphasis upon the fact that Afghanistan has become a shelter for radical religious extremists of all sorts and kinds, terrorists fighting against Russia, China, Uzbekistan, Kyrgyzstan and other Central Asian states.

Up to the current moment the Taliban movement has been continuing to remain a principal sponsor of the Islamic movement of Uzbekistan which proceeds with regular intrusions into the territory of the Fergana Valley (we mean Uzbekistan, Kyrgyzstan and Tajikistan); the organization "Hizb-ut-Tahrir" intensifying its sway in the origin is financed by Taliban as well.

In his book D.L.Latifov analyses strategic goals pursued by key players of the anti-terrorist operation in Afghanistan. There are traced the consistent steps of its new leadership which assumed power after Bonn Summit aimed at fortifying the foundations of Afghan statehood, the historic role of Loya Jirga are shown.

Having scrutinized the social relations of Afghanistan the author characterizes the contemporary economic plight in the country, analyses its position and forecasts the prospects of intergovernmental economic cooperation between the Republic of Tajikistan and the Islamic Republic of Afghanistan.

An undoubted interest for the reader will be correlation of potential capabilities of Central Asian states in the post-conflict reconstruction of Afghanistan, problems and hardships on this way, forecasting of cooperation prospects between the near-boundary Tajik regions and Afghan provinces.

There are convincing arguments forwarded by D.L.Latifov running to the effect that in the surroundings of a stabilizing political situation in the country there enlarge the availabilities of cooperation in the spiritual and cultural realm of the two peoples having cultural, historic, linguistic and religious commonality.

The author devotes a special section to the importance in reference to fortification of the Tajik-Afghan border to ensure security not only for Tajikistan, but for the entire Central Asian region either, for the roles of CSTO (Collective Security Treaty Organization) and SCO (Shanghai Cooperation Organization).

The book is written based on numerous sources, critical analysis of published historic, political literature edited both at home and abroad.

The problems dwelt on in the monograph are indisputably interesting and actual for the contemporary reader.

The topicality of this book is more enhanced in view of the actualities shaped after the collapse of the USSR followed by political independence of the Republic of Tajikistan which has acquired a new geopolitical significance for the outside world pursuing a self-sufficient foreign policy of its own.

The author managed to integrally explore political, cultural and economic aspects of the interrelations between the two countries in the surroundings of both states, distinguished with complicated dynamic changes in their interconnection and contradiction.

In Tajikistan they consolidate peace and political stability, pursue the streamline leading to democratization of social life; the tendency towards improvement of social and economic life is observed shifting to gradual permanency; the level of poverty is going down. Peace and concord enable the Republic of Tajikistan to be implementing ambitious hydro-engineering projects, extending the infrastructure for development of external economic links. They started to attach priority importance to an educational reform, development of culture and public health service.

For the latest five years drastic changes took place in Afghanistan. Due to the anti-terrorist operation and the assistance of international community the Taliban movement has been relatively neutralized. The government of national unity was formed, consisting of the representatives of different ethnic, political forces of the country and foreign Diasporas. Public foundations have been strengthened—they adopted the Constitution of the country, elected the President and the Parliament (Loya Jirga). They established public administration, national army and national security service. Hamid Karzai's government seeks to consolidate political forces of society, being supported by world community is got down to post-conflict reconstruction of the country.

What about a direct cooperation and interrelations between the Republic of Tajikistan and the Islamic Republic of Afghanistan in the spheres of economy, politics and culture after the collapse of the USSR?

The author of the research not only made an endeavor to answer this and other questions, but tracing thoroughly complex contradictory events he gives an assessment of the new shaping situation. He analyses the alignment of political forces and—what is fairly important—expounds his own recommendations on adjustment of long-term, mutually profitable cooperation for a perspective in the interests of post-war reestablishment of Afghanistan and its further development.

Operating with convincing facts and arguments the researcher showed how the potential and needs of the contiguous areas of Tajikistan and Afghanistan can be used effectively in the interests of multilateral economic cooperation; he defined new availabilities of extending and consolidation of infrastructure to establish business cooperation.

Exploration of the contemporary history of bilateral Tajik-Afghan and multilateral regional ties with Afghanistan is of practical importance.

At that the author surveys Tajik-Afghan relations not separately and not under an exclusively descriptive angle, but makes their presentation against a broad historic background.

Thus, for the first time in the modern historical and political science of Tajikistan the author has made an endeavor to scientifically research in integrity interconnection and cooperation between the two neighboring countries in dynamics and contradictions which befell the latest years.

Universal analysis and estimation of economic, cultural and spiritual, political potentials of cooperation between the two countries from the viewpoint of their more effective usage for the sake of Tajik and Afghan nations will enable to lay scientific and practical grounds to develop a policy which would pursue long-term, stable, good-neighborly relations.

The given book will be of great interest not only for political scientists, diplomats, historians, journalists-international law experts, students of international relations departments, but for a wide circle of readers as well.

Mansur BOBOKHONOV,
Doctor of History, Professor
2007.Dushanbe.

INTRODUCTION

Situated in the Middle East, Afghanistan is important in terms of population, well-being of the country, possession of natural resources, as well as of its geographic and geostrategic location.

The situation around Afghanistan has already been in the spotlight of politicians, historians, Mass Media all over the world for more than two decades. Soon after 11 September, 2001 the interest in the developments of this country and their impact on other Central Asian states grew rapidly.

Like other independent states of Central Asia, Afghanistan is going through a very important stage of its statehood development.

Yet, among the most burning issues are those concerning internal development of Afghanistan itself which resulted in stormy disturbances within the country during the last 60-70 years of its history. In-depth study of domestic processes makes it possible to conclude that Afghanistan will more likely remain a hotbed of social, national and religious tension and the world community will have to be dealing with a problem of Afghan adjustment unless an anti-terrorist operation in the country is completed, legal, democratic and fair principles of country administration are developed, which could ensure equality of the peoples and free development of this long-suffering country.

The country proceeds with fighting against terrorism, extremism and drug trafficking. The threat on the part of terrorist forces and gang formations has substantially diminished but not yet eliminated completely. The strikes initially delivered upon Taliban detachments on the part of the Northern Alliance, significant detriment caused by the coalition forces to Taliban and Al-Qaida in the course of anti-terrorist operations made them regroup their forces and shift to guerilla war. The threat of their erosion and revival is still not removed from the agenda. The reason for this lies in the activities of separate political forces of Afghanistan who are trying to make a kind of game with the former governors as if searching for the ways of national reconciliation. The same is the policy of Pakistan and its allies who proceed with the adequate policy in regard to the mentioned extremist organizations in order to account for their presence both in Afghanistan and the entire region being eager to carry into effect regulation of conflicts governed by them.

Therefore, it is necessary to take into account the influence of external forces, strategic goals and the actions of key players of the anti-terrorist operation in Afghanistan, the policy of contiguous states in respect of the processes occurring in the country.

The international coalition against terrorism in Bonn, the United Nations along with the sensible political groups of then-Afghanistan with the support of international community laid the foundations of interim government and identified the future steps for revival of the country, achievement of peace and national reconciliation. The peoples of Afghanistan who had been suffering in those abominable days of their history and sustaining the lasting bloody war equally rejected all former regimes, some citizens giving preference to none of them. They were disappointed by the dictatorship of the republican system established by Mohammad Daoud, Nur Taraki, Hafizulla Amin and by that of the communist pro-Soviet government of Babrak Karmal and his successor Najibullah.

For this reason the historic decisions of Bonn Conference in 2001 regarding the principle of future political structure of Afghanistan were accepted by the majority of the long-suffering peoples of Afghanistan with great enthusiasm. In accordance with the Bonn Agreement the final form of state authority was established only after the new Constitution was drawn up and adopted 18 months after the Emergency Loya Jirga had finished its work. It is quite in the nature of things that Afghan leaders representing different political and ethnic trends having convened in December 2001 in Bonn agreed to hold Loya Jirga as a means of stimulating broad discussions and achieving consensus in future authority structure of Afghanistan after the collapse of the authoritarian regime of the Taliban movement.

Conducting of the two historic Loya Jirgas, adoption of the Fundamental Law, presidential elections, and finally, parliamentary elections in September 2005 in Afghanistan became important milestones in the history of strengthening the statehood fundamentals of the country.

The above-mentioned Loya Jirga was considered emergency, since unlike the elections of previous years when delegates had been appointed by the ruling circles being an object of political manipulations, now the peoples of Afghanistan elected the members of the Parliament by voting which is the factor of democratic development.

It is common knowledge that the national question has been the one taking central place in the political life of the country. A great progress in resolving of this issue was made at Bonn Conference when identifying the national composition of the Interim Authority of Afghanistan.

Therefore, the peculiarity of the Emergency Loya Jirga was marked with the fact that counter to the prevailed Pashtun composition of the national assembly not corresponding to the ethnic structure of the country's population now the elections were held with having taken into consideration a proportional correlation in reference to population in each province. This was the only possibility for putting an end to infinite disputes on quantitative domination of Tajiks or Pashtuns in the country.

The Emergency Loya Jirga introduced such an order which made no provision for monopolization of authority on the part of any personality, party, tribe or region, on the one hand, and created conditions for active and free participation of all social layers, tribes and groups of population in authority and decision making process, on the other hand.

In a word, the decisions of Loya Jirga followed by adoption of the Constitution (Fundamental Law) through general voting laid the foundations which would prevent from reiteration of errors of the past and enable the country to achieve national unity.

The economic life of post-conflict Afghanistan is characterized by the crisis of all branches of economy, devastation and plunder of industrial enterprises, power plants, construction industry and gas pipelines which were left by the pro-Soviet regime of the People's Democratic Party of Afghanistan as well as by price increase for foodstuffs and goods supplemented by the devaluation of the Afghan currency. The above-mentioned processes resulted in impoverishment of the population, crimes wave and corruption piercing the entire hierarchy of power from bottom to the top. Having no availabilities to normally run in agricultural industry because of mined lands, lack of tractors and draft animals, the inhabitants of Afghan villages were forced to grow opium poppy.

The Interim Authority headed by Hamid Karzai which was elected after the Taliban had been defeated requested the world community to assist in the revival of the country's economy. Central authorities were to start everything anew: to organize relevant state structures, economic planning, reconstruction of the demolished infrastructure, staff training, construction of large scale entities so necessary for the functioning of economy, to resolve security problems. At the Summits of the Heads of States-donors which took place in Bonn and Tokyo it was decided to allocate necessary several-stage financial aid for the postwar reconstruction of Afghanistan.

For the last 10 years Tajikistan and other Central Asian states have been closely and consistently cooperating with one another with one goal in mind: to achieve national reconciliation in Afghanistan. They already have had experience in peacemaking.

Today, with the establishment of relative peace within the long-suffering Afghan land, the states of the region are able to use their scientific and technical, economic and cadre potentials for economic recovery of neighboring Afghanistan both on multilateral and bilateral bases. After all, stability in Central Asian states depends much on the stability in neighboring Afghanistan. After the April Revolution of 1978 cooperation of Soviet republics with Afghanistan was confined within the framework of the allied Ministry of external economic links of the USSR. It bore the nature of unilateral gratis aid. That period brought a great experience of multifaceted economic, scientific and technical cooperation among the constituent subjects of the USSR—union republics.

Being a member of the USSR, the Republic of Tajikistan starting from 1985 initiated an establishment of patronage between the Gorno-Badakhshan, Kurgan-Tyube, Kulob regions of Tajikistan and Badakhshan, Balkh, Takhar and Kunduz provinces of Afghanistan that opened a new prospect in the promotion of relations between the neighboring countries. Such products as hydraulics, cable devices, spare parts for cars, chemical fertilizers and commercial mechanical engineering products were exported from Tajikistan to Afghanistan.

When the People's Democratic Party of Afghanistan was in power the relations between our countries were mainly reduced to interparty contacts as well as to cultural, educational and scientific cooperation.

The emergence of Mujahideen and Taliban, their rise to power in Afghanistan along with the policy of terrorism and religious extremism pursued complicated and brought to nothing the cooperation of the neighboring Central Asian states with Afghanistan.

Soon after commencement of the anti-terrorist operation in Afghanistan and Taliban exodus from the political arena, the Central Asian states shifted their political ends towards Afghanistan. At that these states were guided by common regional interests being members of such unions as Eurasian Economic Community, CIS, SCO, as well as OIC and ECO, of which Afghanistan is a member too.

The USA, European countries and the world community altogether are concerned with the problems of post-conflict reconstruction of Afghanistan when relative peace and national reconciliation have been established.

It is next to impossible to attain reconstruction of Afghanistan without removal of drug crime threat both for the state itself and for the contiguous Central Asian region and the entire world as a whole.

It is well known that Afghanistan today is not only the primary producer of drug raw stock, but also a place for their distribution which greatly concerns world community.

Only in 2000 the production of opium in the country amounted to more than the half of the entire volume produced in the world. According to the United Nations, in the mid-1990s when the Taliban came to power in Afghanistan 130.000 acres of land were occupied with opium poppy. To 2000 these squares increased up to 2000 thousand acres.

Primarily Talibs needed resources for the purchase of arms; they supported the production and realization of drugs. For the country ruined by the war with its mass unemployment opium became the only livelihood.

The entire population beginning with farmers right up to state officials turned out to be engaged in drug traffic. If you count the amount of drug stuffs withdrawn across the Tajik-Afghan border only for the last three years the quantum of heroin could have converted over 10 million people on the planet into drug addicts.

This circumstance not only alarms Central Asian states, China, Iran and other countries having a lengthy contiguous border with Afghanistan, but it causes suspicion making them be watchful of the neighboring country. In can't help telling upon political relations either, foreign partners are not sure in what concerns investments of programs and projects on reconstruction of Afghanistan.

Illegal drugs circulation is one of the sources of international terrorism and religious extremism too. In the appeals dealing with the necessity of consolidating the forces of international community the President of the Republic of Tajikistan Emomali Rahmon when making speeches from the tribunes of UNO and other international forums told that a settlement of Afghan crisis in view of liquidation of drug threat proceeding from Afghanistan is inseparably connected with transnational criminality.

Alongside with economic, social and spiritual consequences drug addiction has a sway upon political life of society. Thus, at present corruption and bribery have been thriving as never before in the Afghan society. High-ranking state officials, former military commanders having been bereft of their posts today and getting low salaries purchase tremendous pieces of land, build multi-storied mansions, buy automobiles of foreign models and divers estate property. It is not difficult to guess that this becomes possible due to financial support on the part of drug criminals who contrive to obtain fabulous profits from drug trafficking.

They widely resort to drug trafficking for attainment of political purposes, financing of anti-state or oppositional movements, bribing of officials, co-optation of their people into the parliament, legislative and executive bodies through which respective resolutions and instruments are lobbied for the sake of their own mercenary motives.

According to official statistics, today, five years later after the commencement of the anti-terrorist operation in Afghanistan, even in the capital, to say nothing of the outskirts, terrorist acts, murders, plunders and other criminal events have not been ceasing. Criminal groupings of Taliban and Al-Qaida contrive to penetrate into the country through the Pakistani-Afghan corridor stretching from Pakistani Belujistan to the Afghan provinces of Zabul, Urozgan, Kandahar and Helmand; Uigur separatists move through the Chinese-Afghan plot; militants from Uzbek Movement of Uzbekistan and the Uzbek Jihad go through the Afghan-Uzbek border and other passages of the border.

Thereby, the issues concerned with the fortification of the state frontier are of importance both for Afghanistan and Central Asian states. Therefore the author devotes a part of his research to the review of pressing problems related, in particular, to the situation on the Tajik-Afghan border.

CHAPTER 1

Situation in the Islamic State of Afghanistan and Strategic Goals of Key Players of Anti-terrorist Operation

The starting point of the process concerned with the new formation of the Afghan state is considered the inter-Afghan "Agreement on Interim Mechanisms in Afghanistan up to Reinstatement of Permanently Functioning Governmental Institutions" struck in December 5, 2001 in Bonn under the auspices of UNO. The Bonn Agreement which is similar to "a road-map" of political and economic revival of Afghanistan fixed the composition and mandate of Interim Authority of the Islamic State of Afghanistan headed by Hamid Karzai for the term of six months. Emergency Loya Jirga (traditional Afghan National Assembly) which was convened in the period of June 10-21, 2002 in Kabul formed the Interim Authority chaired by Hamid Karzai who was granted presidential powers with the right of adoption of legislative instruments.

Loya Jirga, a supreme legislative body, was reinstated by nation-wide referendum the first convocation in October 2003.

General presidential elections were held in October 8, 2004. Hamid Karzai was elected a President. This forerun by setting out of vertical government in the center and in the provinces, disarmament of the population, formation of new national armed forces and law-enforcement structures, arrangements for social and economic reconstruction of the country, reforming of justice system.

Hamid Karzai seeks to administer the country and stabilize the situation by means of the economic and military assistance granted by the USA, its allies and the world community. The resolution of the First Tokyo Summit on allocating financial aid amounting to 2,7 billion USD and that of the Second Summit (ibid) where representatives of 40 states were present on rendering economic support to the Islamic State of Afghanistan for regularization of the situation in the country are not being fully realized [1]. For the time being foreign investors hesitate to put up their capital in Afghanistan owing to instability in the country. Hamid Karzai regularly visits foreign states requesting them to speed up the process of granting of promised aid. Neighboring states, as India, Iran and others allocated appreciable gratis aid to Kabul.

After the session of the Organization of Economic Cooperation in Istanbul its delegation visited Kabul having reviewed the economic support programs. Muhsin Aminzade—deputy of the branch Minister of Iran visited Kabul to study the situation, availabilities for future cooperation and the issues related to rendering of financial assistance to the neighboring country.

A great number of nongovernmental organizations (NGOs) established with the support of international organizations can be observed in the country. Different international organizations are seeking to implement all kinds of projects through those NGOs. Unfortunately, the projects are usually managed by persons having little experience and competence. All this is resulting in corruption, abuse and non-targeted use of allocated resources.

A number of state and private independent Mass Media agencies were established in the country. More than 130 independent editions, information services and television are operating within the country. The Government is seeking to establish legitimacy and stability through them, to prevent violation of order, infringement of women's rights and to support development of entrepreneurship.

It should be stated, however, that the government has been confronting more and more difficulties. Clannish behavior, ethnic disunity, nepotism, boundless lawlessness of the former field commanders who went underground and militants of the Taliban breed all sorts of impediments on this way. In fact, it is hard to talk about the spread of the authority of Hamid Karzai, legitimacy and order beyond the center of Kabul.

Under the veil of war against terrorism definite groups behave outrageously, reckon with unwanted persons and seize personnel of international organizations as hostages. Local commanders abandon themselves to mutual squabbles using fire.

Al-Qaida forces and Taliban units went underground, dissolved in the mass waging a guerilla war. It is known that in the course of the anti-terrorist activities only two out of ten Bin Laden's brothers-in-arms were killed. Umar, Mansur, Mullahs Dadalla Sayyaf and others are alive, hiding on the territory between Afghanistan and Pakistan in the vicinity of Chitral. There is a sort of information running to the effect that Sayyaf joined his forces with Hekmatyar. Sayyaf even managed to nominate himself in parliamentary elections and obtain a deputy's seat. It should be noted that there are few Taliban, in the true sense of the word, implying "trained students" present in this movement. The overwhelming majority, even of the command staff, consists of former mujahideen having no religious education and who before the entry to Taliban movement belonged to different groupings. Some of them were forced to become members of the Taliban movement [2]. Simply stated, the Taliban have not been liquidated yet; they have just redeployed. Some of them have already returned to Kabul as refugees. Others set up their staff in Badakhshan, Jalalabad, Kandahar and other provinces on the border with Pakistan as well as on its territory. Leader of the Taliban movement Mullah Umar called his compatriots for Jihad against Americans. He appointed Mullah Abdullah as Commander-in-Chief of the resistance forces. Al-Qaida terrorists murdered a group of government forces in Helmand province. They spread leaflets all over Kandahar among education employees menacing the latter with killing if they didn't cease to work for the new government. Armed conflicts regularly take place between them and government forces in southern provinces.

US Ambassador in Kabul Robert Finn ascertained that the Taliban and Al-Qaida forces became active within the territories which are on the border with Pakistan and stated that Pakistan ought to control and suppress the subversive activities of extremists.

The Government seeks to organize national armed forces. At the present there are contingents of American, English, Dutch, Turkish and other forces in the country. Taking into account the fact that the Afghans had lost their military personnel for the last 25 years of war, Germans and Englishmen got down to training military servicemen in Afghanistan. They are also trained abroad. The Government set up the Academy under the Ministry of Interior.

The US Military Command took a commitment to train 20 thousand professional military servicemen within one and a half years and to create a 70-thousand efficient army by the year 2009. During his visit to Dushanbe in January 2003 Hamid Karzai stated that he would hail the deployment of military servicemen from Tajikistan within the international contingent in Afghanistan. The Republic of Tajikistan agreed to train military personnel of junior officers for Afghanistan.

As a total, national security is expected to be provided by forces of 7 corps with 6000 servicemen in each and to quarter them within the whole territory of the country.

The Northern Alliance presented by Tajiks in connection with the political results of its whirlwind attack and seizure of 90 % of the country's territory displeased both the USA and Pakistan because it destroyed their plans on formation of the puppet pro-Pashtun Government. Great doubts arose primarily as to the functioning of powerful government that Hamid Karzai hoped to build up in view of the difficulties related to a potential attainment of consensus between such notorious figures being influential for that moment as Fakhim, Abdul Rashid Dostum and Ismael Khan each of whom not only had a foreign sponsor of his own, but controlled the entrusted territory with a respective ethnic representation. Karzai managed to achieve such consensus having offered each of them high posts in his Government.

Another fact causing apprehension is that the Taliban withdrew too rapidly, in an organized manner, as if it was a scheduled action. All these precarious circumstances make one hesitate as to whether the anti-terrorist action in Afghanistan is really moving to its alleged accomplishment.

Owing to the commencement of military actions in Iraq, the situation in Afghanistan has aggravated in favor of Hamid Karzai's opponents as the credit of confidence on the part of electorate started decreasing. The reason for it is as follows: after having invoked compatriots residing abroad many Afghans started returning to Afghanistan from Pakistan, Iran, Central Asian states, Europe. Soon after the terrorist acts in London the above-mentioned states (3 million refugees remaining in Pakistan; about 1 million being in Iran) passed resolutions prescribing Afghan refugees to leave their country.

At present acute problems are arisen already for the first generation of refugees, since they needed to be provided with housing, jobs and social rehabilitation. Those 150-200 thousand refugees who returned to Afghanistan were allocated lands by the government for construction purposes, but they do not have adequate funds for procurement of expensive building materials.

Bureaucracy, corruption, lack of order and guarantees of security for citizens, endless facts of lawlessness, violation, robberies, drug crimes and murders cause disappointment of population and shatter confidence to the Government of the country which faces difficulties in implementing its pre-election program. Public and Parliament's majorities express dissatisfaction with the activities of the Government [3].

So, we proceed with strategic goals of the players of the anti-terrorist operation in Afghanistan.

The key player of the anti-terrorist operation in Afghanistan—the United States of America—pursues both external and internal targets.

To the internal targets there refer such problems which are distinctly observed in the USA:

- decline in country's economy, setback in production and slowdown of its growth rate, struggle for influence between USD and EURO, decrease in degree of consolidation of the society, increase in immoral events, and at last, unconcealed allergy of the majority of the countries of world community towards the foreign policy of the United States. The terrorist acts of 11 September though—however cynically it may sound—especially "Retribution" operation didn't enable to settle these problems, but they "froze" their further development either.

As for the external targets of the USA, one of the most important of them was to restore their status of "chief arbitrator' and "major guarantor" of international security that is to prolong the situation of one-polar world with a dominating role of the USA.

The declared war with international terrorism under the auspices of the USA, their firm determination to take naked possession of Iraq in spite of public opinion made it possible to consolidate around them serve a part of the world community.

Afghanistan being chosen as the first object of forceful ascendancy is no fortuitous factor. *Firstly*, in world community's opinion it really looked out as "a breeding-ground for international terrorism" and a base for dissemination of drugs. Accordingly, contempt of the international law could not produce intense negative reaction. *Secondly*, by sly degrees it was possible to resolve the no less important strategic objective—to build up a pro-American government in this country and its attachment in Central Asian region. Hence ensured alternative routes for conveyance of Caspian petroleum evading Russia could be of avail.

At last, not to allow or at least weaken the opportunities of emergence of states or a coalition of states which could challenge the influence of the USA in the region.

As for the interests of Russia, it should be defined what Afghanistan was for the Russian Federation in the context of its Central Asian policy. Afghanistan was traditionally considered by the authoritative elite as some kind of buffer from external influence in the southern direction. And for the decade passed it was seen as potential key factor in case of emergency concerned with exercising influence over Central Asian republics.

Soon after the victory of Islamic radical movements in Afghanistan there arose a threat of expansion concerned with the influence of Islamic revival in the states of Central Asia with Moslem population, but the arc of Islamic radical movement curved inwards in regard to CIS territory. The border with unstable far abroad has approached Russia.

Preservation of status-quo in Afghanistan, regardless of all disadvantages connected with terrorism and drug trafficking, ensured, some guarantees against spreading of the Afghan conflict zone over Central Asia, on the one hand, and provided transportation of hydrocarbon resources of the region (Uzbekistan, Turkmenistan and Kazakhstan) through the territory of Russia, on the other hand.

However, the existing status-quo began to fail with a commencement of anti-terrorist operation and actual involvement of Russia and other Central Asian states in it. In this situation Russia faced a serious dilemma: on the one hand, it could not help participating in the anti-terrorist operation; on the other hand, it did not agree with the nature of the operation and its orientation, namely, initial indications to "Islamic trace" of terrorist acts in the USA and the prospects of the USA being enhanced in Central Asia.

Russia was searching for a way out of the complex situation and was successful in having found it.

Firstly, having become one of the leaders of the international antiterrorist coalition (which increased the level of Russian influence in the world) Russia managed to improve its rather clouded relationships with the USA. The United States realize that the Afghan problem cannot be resolved without participation of Russia.

Secondly, the position of Russia coordinated with the partners from Central Asian region as well as with the leaderships of China, India and Iran enabled the country to avoid needless confrontation and not to spoil relations not only with its strategic allies but with the Moslem world either.

Thirdly, Russia was recognized by world community as an influential world center of force; the most important factor being the voice of Western countries in this unanimous chorus.

After all, Russians seem to realize that the presence of several American military bases in the region is not valuable military presence at all. Moreover, military intervention into the affairs of Iraq complicates not only the situation in Afghanistan but the very further sojourn of Americans in the region. The struggle against terrorism will cost the USA dear (about 100 billion USD) apart from human losses.

In 2002 Elizabeth Johns, former Deputy State Secretary of the USA declared that the United States were not intended to have military bases in Central Asia. However, in 2005, by declaring of the probability of struggle against terrorists and extremists in Afghanistan, she confuted her own words. As is well known, Americans deployed their military bases in Kyrgyzstan and Uzbekistan at that time.

Of course, ATO itself and its prolonged retardation unfavorably tell upon Russia and Russian sway over Central Asia, especially if the USA has been bogging down in Afghanistan with no views for a tangible end—but it is a different issue. Americans will not only change the geopolitics in the region, but they will bring ATO and Atlantic Alliance participants to disruption.

The position of China adheres to the slant that US intervention in Afghan conflict (as it happened with Iraq) in any form breaks the geostrategy of China which beginning from the late 1980s, is expressed in the following formula: "to rely on the North; to stabilize western direction, to concentrate main efforts in the East and the South".

Until recent time this strategy was quite successful. China managed to accede to strategic agreements with its northern neighbors. China even succeeded in getting hold of some territories (of Kazakhstan, Kyrgyzstan and Tajikistan) that could not have been achieved when these countries were members of the USSR. Furthermore, China became one of the constituents of the regional security system.

Until 2002 China maintained positive relations with Pakistan, India, NATO and even with the Taliban. Now such a fragile balance has been disturbed. At that it is not inconceivable that the pro-American puppet Government will consolidate in Afghanistan which is extremely undesirable for China having pains with "Sintzyan Problem". It is no mere chance that there was initiative in SCO Summit of July 2005 to demand from USA so that they would determine the period for withdrawal of military bases from Central Asia.

China has also well pleaded claims against the US foreign policy. In Beijing they consider that there should not be double standards in struggle against international terrorism. If the USA is really willing "to do away with this evil", first of all, it should reconsider its strategy in respect of Taiwan, Tibet and Sintzyan. It is no secret that Americans did not convey captured militants of Al-Qaida to Guantanamo (Cuba). They keep them in special camps on the territory of Pakistan for special purposes.

It is obvious for Beijing that ethnic separatism resorts to terrorism for attainment of its political goals. This fact is evidenced by the terrorist acts against Chinese diplomats committed on 25 February 2003 in Beijing and later on in Bishkek. In this respect, the notions "ethnic separatists" and "terrorists" are both equivalent for China. It is on the strength of this reason that China did not designate so accurately the degree of its participation in ATO. After the commencement of the anti-terrorist operation Beijing fortified its western borders, including those ones with Afghanistan [4].

As for economic interests, Chinese People's Republic has been intensively and successfully possessing Afghan market. The country is flooded with cheap Chinese goods in literal sense.

Chinese companies won 5 bids as contractors of projects on construction of highways. Experts underline that Chinese workers provide more qualitative construction assembly works and that Chinese labor force is cheaper as compared to Turks.

Chinese penetration into Afghanistan hardly suits the USA. However, the United States could not prevent this. Pakistan probably supports China in its activities within Afghanistan, since China presumes it is in competence of supply and Afghans with their low purchasing capacity have certain demands. At that China is not getting involved in political processes yet, but successfully develops the market and expands its influence in economy. It will probably be a good background for the further transformation of economic influence into a political one.

The targets of Pakistan are seen rather distinctly.

Firstly, it is vital for Pakistan to retain influence in Afghanistan.

Secondly, it is important for Pakistan to enter closest relations with the USA and resolve its economic problems.

Thirdly, "to save its face" before the Islamic world.

Fourthly, to consolidate its position in the forming alliances of Central Asian region (along with the entry to the Organization of Islamic Conference and ECO Pakistan in 2005, with the support of China, attained its participation as an observer in SCO as well).

As early as 1995 Minister of Foreign Affairs of Pakistan Sardar Asif Ahmad making a speech in Lahore (Punjab province) stated that their foreign policy priorities would be based upon development of all-round relations with Central Asian states. Prior to these events, yet in 1994 they had been working out a conception of joint responsibility of Pakistan and Uzbekistan for Central Asian region security, especially in Tajikistan (for Uzbekistan) and in Afghanistan (for Pakistan).

The force which boiled in the Afghan-Pakistani kettle (detachments of Talibs who have shaved their beards join successfully in the new Afghan society and adapt themselves in it they nominated over 7 candidates out of former Taliban government at the parliament elections in September 2005) will overlap the scales of American interests in the region. This force is able to start up the process of regional transformation more than of afghan one. This firstly applies to reshaping, secondly, to transport communications and thirdly to energy communications of the central part of Eurasian continent.

Iran desires that the anti-terrorist operation in neighboring Afghanistan did not cause social disruptions and breakdown of political regime. For the time being it manages to regulate this balance; it is accounted for by its union with Russia to which Iran clings to a more extent.

It is historically known that Iran exerts influence upon the population residing on the vast territories of Afghanistan (Mashhad, Herat, Balkh, Mazar-i-Sharif) through the community of language, religion and history. Iran, just like Pakistan, is interested in retaining influence in Afghanistan through its protégés in the new Government and Parliament.

It appears that Iran is conducting a two-track policy in respect of presence of the USA in the region. The struggle against former opponent Saddam Hussein and his overthrow respond to Iranian interests, being a kind of platform upon which the interests of Iran and the USA coincide. However, Iran is not confident that on having entered Afghanistan and Iraq, Americans wouldn't get back at the next country in the same manner, i.e. with Iran which is in the black list of the states referred to the "Evil Axis".

All the more so since over 500 Al-Qaida followers had in due time entrenched in Iran who were recently arrested and deported from country.

If as a result of ATO in Afghanistan persons welcome to Iran (those who headed Ministry of Defense, Ministry of Foreign Affairs and some other Ministries), occupied seats in the Government, it is quite possible that a pro-American leader might come to power in Iraq from the opponents of its former administration which promises to be not so good for the Eastern neighbor.

Adverse development of situation in Afghanistan related to instability of the anti-Taliban coalition in overcoming inner divergences caused the change of geopolitical situation in Central Asia for the new independent states. The anti-Taliban alliance was losing its key advantage of existence as a buffer for the indopendent national republics of Central Asia—that of an absence of political risks and necessity to bear serious material and military expenses [5].

To cease conflict in Afghanistan is the main objective of Central Asian states in ATO.

The matter is that in recent few years there observed an omniscient rollback and an indirect participation in ATO in Afghanistan conducted under the auspices of the USA. It implies, first of all, that the USA will temporarily not bring up the problem of democracy and human rights in these countries that opens broad possibilities both in respect to consolidating existing regimes and fighting against opposition.

Secondly, financial aid received from the USA for providing their territories for conducting land and air operations makes it possible for those countries "to patch up" the gaps in the budgets of Central Asian states.

Thus, US Defense Minister Donald Rumsfeld during his visit to Dushanbe in 2005 promised the President of the Republic of Tajikistan Emomali Rahmon to render financial assistance in implementation of several projects as well as in overcoming the consequences of natural hazards which are so characteristic for the mountainous republic, in facilitating training of personnel etc.

During his regular visit to Tajikistan in July 2006 US Defense Ministry D. Rumsfeld promised to assist in implementation of hydraulic power projects, construction of power transmission lines from Tajikistan to Pakistan via the territory of Afghanistan as well as in completion of the construction of bridges. His visit turned out to be a continuation of cooperation in the frameworks of the struggle against international terrorism and drug-trafficking [6].

According to official data in 2004 the USA invested in the Republic of Tajikistan about 52 per cent out of the total amount of all the capitals invested. Moreover, the greater part of humanitarian aid which Tajikistan received from abroad was donated by the USA.

The so called "Uncle Sam" with its generosity could not have helped shattering the steadfastness of the states sustaining a really hard plight caused by the long-lasting slump of economy. In Kyrgyzstan Donald Rumsfeld articulated the allocation of lump-sum aid for this country to the amount of 200 million dollars and further annual grants on the part of the USA.

Thirdly, ATO being anti-Islamic in its essence enables once and forever to settle accounts with the religious opposition. In reference to Russia and China the USA may become an alternative force in the region.

At the same time one should not miss the fact that the principal element of the strategy in regard to the war with terrorism declared by the USA is a bereavement of immunity related both to terrorists and the country suspected of "cultivation" of terrorist organizations on its territory or having contact with the latter as well.

Since the war with terrorism promises to be a prolonged one the prospects of intensification of terrorism on the territory of Central Asia (especially in the actualities of the large-scaled operation in Afghanistan) are predictable enough, only this very circumstance converts Central Asian states into the hostages of the given strategy.

Since military operations in Iraq militants from Taliban and Al-Qaida detachments entrenched both in Pakistan and Afghanistan having taken advantage of the coalitional forces being diverted in the direction of Iraq invoked extremist actions against the power of Hamid Karzai in 2007. There is no guarantee that on having fortified their positions in Afghanistan in future they would not undertake "unfriendly" actions against the neighbors supporting the coalition in the issues concerned with ATO.

Any military operation against Afghanistan in future can pour out into a large-scaled conflict in the region, since Central Asian states where the positions of Islam are strong and opposition comes out with unconcealed Islamic programs, turn to be in disfavor. There can exemplify the endeavors of effectuating "poppy" and "tulip" revolutions in Kyrgyzstan and Uzbekistan in 2005. After all, it is unknown who is predestined to be the next one in the list of terrorists subsequent to Chechnya militants entered into it. Having supported the USA in the operation "Retribution" Central Asian states not only incur the anger of Talibs, activists and members of Hizb-ut-Tahrir, the Islamic movement of Uzbekistan and the Uzbek Jihad; at the same time these countries lay foundations for activation of their own opposition.

It is not fortuitous that at the meeting with Ambassador Extraordinary and Plenipotentiary of Egypt on the occasion of handing in Credentials in February 18, 2003 the President of Tajikistan Emomali Rahmon emphasized that accusations addressed to Islamic religion under the disguise of divers slogans are utterly unwarranted and Tajikistan would have never admitted of anything which may cause inter-religious conflicts.

As regards the policy pursued by Central Asian states in reference to the events of Afghanistan, it has different varieties in each republic. Coordination or integration of efforts are out of the question, since the relations of each concrete state with another one shape respective of the item vector of both its interrelations with the USA, Russia and of its own domestic political situation as well.

Thereby, the statement running to the effect that a peculiar "anti-terrorist coalition" has formed for the present time is somewhat optimistic.

If not to display foresight and to lose the ability of tracing the reality of rapidly changing situation in the region, to design on the premise of current considerations based on authority of momentary conjunctures in the region we can't exclude a probability in respect of Central Asian states which being involved in ATO and having different interests in the atmosphere of deterioration of inner economic position, enhancement of poverty among population, territorial and ethnic discords in the very region itself [7].

Notes

1. The Middle East at the End of 21st century. Materials of Republican scientific practical conference in Dushanbe. 2003. RTSU Publication, p. 90.
2. Davydov A.D. Afghanistan. Talibs Looking Forward to Assume Power.//Asia and Africa, 2001, No. 7
3. Asia-Plus, July 13, 2006, No. 28 (338).
4. See: Afghanistan at Transitional Stage (September 2001-June 2002). M. 2002 ASTI Printing-house, p. 184-193
5. Ahmad Rashid. Taliban: Islam, Petroleum and New Big Games in Central Asia. I.B. Tauris, 2001
6. Mellat, July 13, 2006 No. 27 (45).
7. "The Middle East at the End of the 20th—at the Beginning of the 21st Centuries" RTSU Publication, Dushanbe, 2003. p. 69

CHAPTER 2

Strengthening of Afghan Statehood Foundations And Its International Importance

Paragraph 1. The Historic Role of Loya Jirga in the Life of Afghan Society

Jirga in Afghanistan is traced back to ancient history. Its age incepts in the times of the ancient Afghan society, it may even be regarded as its satellite. The ancestors of modern Afghans recognized it as a social value, a political and judicial agency since the centuries passed; this recognition being preserved up to nowadays.

With the development of social life, while political order was being enforced, the state needed a sort of a national democratic medium of governance in order to ensure the interests of the masses. This very need preconditioned formation of local Jirga in certain areas where people resided. They were caused by the urgency of the time responding to national problems bound to be resolved. Therefore they played an important historic role [1].

The vitality of Jirga, its compliance to urgent political and social needs of the ancient Afghan society was accounted for by its being based on a unique deliberative principle when ethno-clan-tribal problems were to be resolved on the grounds of local community governance; thus Jirga acquired the right of a local legislative body.

Jirga appeared in the period of the communal-tribal system when the most important problems of tribal life were solved at common gatherings. Further on the feudalized top elite of Afghan tribes resorted to such gatherings in their class interests. With the rise of the Afghan state the intertribal Grand Jirga had been gradually turning into an element of public administration [2].

Afghans single out two types or two levels of Jirga:

1. Sabha Jirga (national meeting)
2. Samti Jirga (meeting of authorities).

Sabha Jirga assembles to address local social issues concerned with one village or clan. All who wish may take part in it, women inclusive. At that any participant can openly express his/her opinion. But no voting takes place. Adoption of solutions is not based on the principle of a greater number of voters; every family may be represented by any number of its members, so a quantum of participants in Jirga is not limited.

Jirga is convened when there raise the problems requiring common settlement. These may be the issues related with politics, law or intertribal relations. If a problem of this sort springs up inside the village community the heads of all families belonging to the latter gather to discuss jointly possible ways of settling the conflict. If the issue concerns the members of other communities, they convene Jirga of the clan or sub-tribal Jirga. Discussion at Jirga is going on until not a single objection remains after this or that decision or when each participant realizes that consent is impossible, at least at the present Jirga. When contradictions arise and groups with different points of view spring up their move forward mediators, at that it happens spontaneously, without any official proceedings. They seek to reconcile opinions of groups to settle the divergences on consensus basis.

At Jirga there is no chairman who regulates debates and the authority of the mediator is based not only and rather on his wealth than a sequence of his individual features, such as life experience, age, oratory abilities. More frequently these functions are performed by the spinghirs (the white-bearded)—wise old men. If mediators fail to bring the participants' opinions to "common denominator" a meeting stops going on and solution of the arguable issue is postponed for a new convocation of the council or they simply never return to the issue of disagreement [3].

The principal purpose of Jirga is to achieve regulated interrelations between one clan members and a unity as to the solution of the problems addressed.

The most essential function of Jirga, in military branch especially, is addressing of the issues related to outward ties of a clan and a tribe. This function is performed by Samti Jirga not including all at a running but only highly authoritative members of a tribal organization—spinghirs and prominent authorities of the Moslem clergy.

J. Spain characterizes this aspect of Jirga activity as follows: "Jirga has a function which may be titled as foreign affairs. It is Jirga which listens to a state agent or a representative of the other tribe that wishes to discuss the problem concerned with both parties. Jirga can also assign a representative for an intertribal Jirga, for negotiations with the government or inform a foreigner of this or that issue.

Its representatives are not free being only Jirga's tools pursuing its instructions" [4]. In the course of the durable historic period all the governance in the country was implemented through Jirgas which played the role of legislative bodies as well as advocated social interests of civilians. Thus, the role of Jirga in regulating of social life, ensuring of unity and consent has been increasing, since the fortune of any human being depends on the social environment of his habitation and so it exercises influence upon his/her behavior.

Members of communities having faced the difficulties and contradictions of their milieu strive for their overcoming. These aspirations and intentions of people are conducive in the matter of solidifying interaction and cooperation between the members of communities. Jirgas as legal and social subjects played an efficacious role in regulating of social life, assisting to surmount hardships emergent.

A striking feature of the centuries-old history of the national Jirga is a leading role of an individual in it. Alongside with the grey-bearded much younger people are included in it; never did it obey any personality, even the most influential one. All the members of Jirga can freely participate in discussions of problems and vindicate their opinion on equal footing [5].

Customs and traditions of Jirga are relatively developed and its resolutions in spite of communal-clan peculiarities are perceived with esteem by everyone. These customs and traditions are relatively developed among Pashtun nomadic tribes of Afghanistan. They serve as an important medium when clan-tribal clashes are to be settled. Decisions and recommendations are obligatorily accepted by community and the society on the whole [6].

The principle of equality is displayed in the proceedings observed when there is an assemblage of Jirga, at a tribe gathering everyone can express his opinion as all the members enjoy equal rights.

There exist Jirgas of clan, village or nomadic communities, those of tribes and sub-tribes etc. However, there is nothing of hierarchy in it, i.e. there are no higher instances or supreme councils. Jirga is convened when the issues requiring common decision arise.

Jirga can settle tribal disputes due to the principle inherent in it. It is not only a medium of solution concerned with social problems in community but with all other vital problems either. These may be the matters referring to intertribal relations. Invoking spiritual authorities Jirga determines criteria for condemnation of perpetrators and their punishment.

This council is convened upon requests of both influential authorities of community and any member of it either when a corresponding situation and topic arises. Failure to participate in its activity is imposed with tax.

On gathering at Council in a mosque or under the shade of trees people argue on essential problems of self-governance and take decisions bound to be followed by everyone. That one who ignores them without a reasonable cause is subjected to a strict punishment—public reprimand [7].

The mentioned Jirgas are compulsory both for nomadic Pashtun tribes and for Tajiks, Turkmens, Uzbeks, Belugis and Nuristanis. Afghans have also other forms of deliberative Jirgas of a higher standard but they are identical with primary national Jirgas.

As for a managerial function of Jirga there prevails settlement of housing problems and other social issues which depend on capability of Jirga and even on individual features of its members.

Every time when Jirga as a primary social base of management protects real national interests it serves for reconciliation, and on the contrary, if it is targeted at the consideration of a narrow minority the decisions passed will bear an exclusively consumer feature. So, there can be principally polar moments.

In his book "The Life of Afghans through Jirga" Mohammad Hayat Khan wrote: "Jirga is a place for open declaration of people's own will" [8]. Local Jirgas are historically recognized as social institutions—basic links of the supreme legislative power.

Invocation to Jirga as a deliberative institution for setting clan-tribal issues is traced back yet to the 16th-17th centuries when Afghans passed to agricultural development and urbanization from the period of migration and commodity relations; the society had been dominated by feudal atmosphere at that time. It was mostly peculiar for Pashtun tribes [9].

The new vitally important social formation promoted to the establishment of feudal state grounds.

In spite of internal discrepancies, aspirations of foreign states aimed at enslaving the Afghan people, Jirgas conduced to solidarity of tribal chiefs and religious authorities in the national liberation movement, to the unity and alliance of tribes against foreign interventionists. In the 16th century (1579) the national liberation movement of enlighteners headed by Boyazid, which established a feudal government, leaning on Khatic ethnic tribes was struggling persistently against Avrangzeb, an Indian conqueror in the period of 1668-1670. Even in these surroundings social and political life of society was regulated through ethnic clan-tribal Jirgas. Fighting with foreign interventionists they defended, first of all, an independence of communities. Therefore, the struggle against foreign intruders was backed with all members of Jirga [10].

It is worth mentioning that ethnic clan-tribal Jirgas in 19th century played a great role in the defense of the independence of the country encroached by foreign invaders. It is evidenced, in particular, by the drives on formation of national armed teams of "mayman" in which the "momban" community took part; it made English colonizers escape not only from Afghanistan but from Hindustan peninsula in general.

The national liberation movement in Afghanistan terminated in 1897 with the defeat of English colonizers [11].

These were clan-tribal Jirgas that manifested heroism and patriotism having contributed greatly into the regularization of the social and political life of society. The Afghan people proved its promptitude to fight against old adversaries—the Englishmen. For a short historic period liberation movement for national independence of Afghanistan in 1919 under the guidance of Qazi Amannullah Khan in Kabul Khanate demonstrated it convincingly in deed.

Evidently vitality and long existence of Jirga in society may be to some extent explained by invocation of religious sources for benediction.

Thus, in Al-Suru of the Koran (ayat 53) the importance and value of Jirga in social life of people are noted. Important social problems concerned with interrelations between Moslems in pursuance with religious values of Islam are solved through the decisions of such organ as Jirga is. For example, the holy book runs: "Those who believe in Allah invoke him for remitting their sins after they perpetrated something not good, hereby they forget about their personal relations with society" [12]. Asking the Almighty prescription the Afghan people solved all important national problems at Jirga. All those who ignored resolutions or acted contrary to it was punished in conformity with Shariat.

Resolutions approved by Jirga council and aimed at strengthening of social ties with public circles played a considerable role in consolidation of people.

An execution of Jirga solutions required a resolute will on the part of society members.

In all social and political structures functioning in the course of millenniums the role and influence of national Jirga are reflected.

It's natural that over thousands years the society can't help remaining without changes in people themselves, in their vocabulary, in state structure, in ethnical culture etc. But in spite of all this Jirga as a solid social structure-forming dominant managed to preserve itself.

In the period after April revolution Jirga was perceived by the authority and the people as one of stable national traditions both at the primary level and at the common national one—everything was regulated by Jirgas and advisory community meetings.

Jirga is recognized by the Afghan society as an important factor of national reconciliation [13].

Through the centuries Loya Jirgas were convened in Afghanistan to elect a new king, to adopt Constitution and to solve other important political issues.

According to the tradition chiefs of tribes and elders took part in the work of Loya Jirga being sent to Kabul by local councils—shuros.

In the past Loya Jirgas were fairly representational meetings. All ethnic and religious groups of Afghanistan sent their delegates there. Women participated in the sessions of "The Grand Council" in 1964 and 1979. In 1977 women averaged already 15 % out of all delegates.

The first Loya Jirga in the history of Afghanistan was held in 1411, they addressed the issue concerned with migration of a group of Pashtun tribes from Kandahar to Peshawar (44 %).

In 1747 Pashtun chieftains gathered in Kandahar to elect a king. His name was Ahmad Shah Durrani; he was the only man who didn't utter a word during the work of Loya Jirga. Later on he founded the state of Afghanistan [14].

In 1841 and 1864 Loya Jirgas considered the issue on a revolt against the British ascendancy.

In 1928 king Amonullah Khan in order to convince deputies in an urgency of reforms in the country asked queen Soraya to put off her paranja in public. This courageous step eventuated into the revolt among Afghan conservatives.

Primarily the Afghan parliament was elected yet under Zahir Shah's constitutional monarchy in 1969. After M. Daoud had been subverted in 1974 Afghanistan was proclaimed to be a republic and in the period when communists assumed power the parliament didn't function; that being the time of Nur Mohammad Taraki in 1979, further on followed by Hafizulla Amin, communists Babrak Karmal and Najibullah. Under the two-month governance of Sigbatullah Mojadeddi, the four-month summer presidency of Prof. B. Rabbani and in the period of Taliban being in power the parliament did not function either.

Thus, the last completely proper Loya Jirga was held in 1973, but after the King Zahir Shah's submergence it was not conducted any more.

In accordance with the Constitution adopted in 1987 and with national and historical traditions Loya Jirga is the supreme manifestation of force and mouthpiece of the will of the people of Afghanistan [15].

It includes:

- members of the National Council;
- 10 persons elected by the people representing each province and administrative unit being on equal footing with it;
- governors and mayor of Kabul;
- Prime Minister, his deputies and members of the Council of Ministers;
- Chairman of the Supreme Court, his deputies and members of the Supreme Court;
- Attorney-general and his deputies;
- Chairman and members of Constitutional Council;
- maximum 50 persons out of notable votaries from realms of politics, culture, science, religion appointed by the President.

The competence of Loya Jirga encompasses:

- adoption of Constitution and making amendments into it;
- election and resignation of the President;
- consent for war declaration;
- passing resolutions on the most important issues related to the national fortune of the country.

In the period of June 11-19, 2002 the All-Afghan Emergency Loya Jirga Assembly took place in Kabul. This forum became an important stage of the postwar state reinstatement in the country through achievement of national consent, formation of stable state authority institutions and steady political regime. The results of Loya Jirga work fortified the course pursuing a resurgence of independent and peaceful Afghanistan, complete liquidation of hotbeds of international terrorism, religious extremism and drug addiction danger on its territory [16].

The process of elections to Loya Jirga was passing in conformity with Bonn Agreement signed on 5 December 2001. In January 2002 on Loya Jirga convocation they formed the special independent commission which defined the regulations and procedures for elections into "The Grand Council" and its further activity.

The elections of Loya Jirga started in April 15, 2002. At the beginning the local councils of elders ("shuros") on the level of counties and municipalities appointed electors whose number depended on a quantum of residents of the given administrative units. After that the electors at polling station situated in regional centers elected the delegates to Loya Jirga from their milieu.

In accordance with Bonn Agreement this Loya Jirga titled as the Emergency Loya Jirga was bound to determine a political system of Afghanistan and lay the grounds for the new Constitution.

Thus at this session of Loya Jirga it was Hamid Karzai whom they validated as the Chairman of the "The Interim Authority of Afghanistan" [17].

1540 delegates from all the provinces of Afghanistan approved the governmental staff and key ministries:

- Ministry of Defense
- Ministry of Interior
- Ministry of Finance
- Ministry of Education
- Ministry of Higher Education
- Ministry of Public Health
- Ministry of Civil Aviation and Tourism
- Ministry of Communications [18].

Loya Jirga assembles in cases of urgent problems of importance in the life of Afghanistan springing up; its convocation is not confined with any time limitations. The quantum of deputies, the people's representatives is limited; it makes up approximately 1500 members from each ethnic group inhabiting the state.

Thus, Loya Jirga became a supreme political and legislative authority encompassing all links of power, settlement of ethnic and clan-tribal clashes, protection of the country, national reconciliation, election of the President, declaration of war in pursuit of the defense of independence.

Notes

1. Mohammad Hayat Khan M. Life of Afghans through Jirga. Kabul, 1954—p. 53
2. Aslanov M. Contemporary Afghanistan. M. 1960. p. 67
3. Afghanistan: History, Economy, Culture. Collection of articles. M. 1989 p. 62
4. Spain J.W. The Way of Pathans. London. 1990. p. 102
5. Beyte E. Afghanistan. M. 1929 p. 71
6. Spain J.W. The Way of Pathans. London. 1990. p. 43
7. The History of Afghanistan. Mysl. M. 1982 p. 366
8. Mohammad Hayat Khan M. Life of Afghans through Jirga. Kabul, 1954—p.140
9. Raysner I.M. Development of Feudalism and Formation of State by Afghans. M. 1954. p. 414
10. Mason V.M., Ramodin V.L. The History of Afghanistan. M. Nauka. p. 121
11. Rishtiya S.K. Afghanistan In the 19th Century. M. Nauka. 1958 p. 125
12. Yavich L.S., Petrov V.S. The Theory of State and Law.Leningrad,1987 p.250
13. Andreyev A., Shumov S. The History of Afghanistan. M. Znaniye,2002. p.147
14. Gubar G.M. Ahmad Shah As the Founder of Afghan State. M. Znaniye, 1959 p. 68
15. The Constitution of the Republic of Afghanistan. Kabul. 1987. p. 26
16. Testing by Jirga//Weekly Journal. 2002, No. 071 p. 59
17. Blinov F. Karzai's Day//Time. 2001/ No.45 p. 4
18. Karzai will Declare Key Ministers//Internet site *www.bbc.uk* p. 51

PARAGRAPH 2

Formation of Contemporary Public
Authority After September 11, 2001

Since mostly ancient times Afghanistan existed as a monarchic state, in early 20th century it developed into a constitutional monarchy and finally, after the armed coup d'etat of 1973 headed by Mohammad Daoud it became a Republic.

This was an important step forward in the cause of building a democratic state. The republican governance of Daoud had been reigning up to April, 27 1978 when as result of the next coup d'etat his place was occupied by the Democratic Republic of Afghanistan.

Political power was transferred to the People's Democratic Party important changes having been in outcome in the political system of Afghanistan. The Revolutionary Council became the Superior Body of State Authority.

According to the Fundamental Law adopted in November 30, 1987 Afghanistan became a presidential republic that told upon its political authority. In the Afghan political circles and in social consciousness as a whole there dominated the comprehension of expediency as to the republican structure established in the country. Hamid Karzai gave preference to creation of a strong presidential power and a one-chamber parliament non-controlled by regional leaders. His opponents from religious parties and regions stood for parliamentary government and limitation of state head's authority. In his respect it is important to note that a part of Pashto population, first of all, insistently stood for the reinstatement of the constitutional monarchy. Ex-king Mohammad Zahir Shah on the eve of the historic Loya Jirga declared his promptitude for being at the head of the state to bring Afghanistan to national reconciliation.

Before dwelling in details on the election fight in reference to the presidential election and its subsequent results one should analyze the poouliarities of national structure and different approaches in regard to ensuring of reasonable balanced combination between Islamic and secular principles in the Afghan society.

The key issue on which the image and vitality of the renovating Afghan statehood will depend is ensuring of its poly-ethnic character.

Afghanistan is a multinational country; the greater part of its population composes Pashtuns, Tajiks, Uzbeks and Hazara. Alongside with them there live over ten other nations. The last two decades are distinguished with cardinal changes in the social and ethnic tissue of the Afghan society; traditional domination of Pashtuns having been undermined.

The organized representatives of Tajiks, Uzbeks, Hazara and other ethnic groups being also imbued with military abilities entered the political stage.

Suffice it to remind that the basic force of the Interim Authority of Afghanistan in Kabul and a number of provinces befell the armed formations of the former anti-Taliban United Front ("Northern Alliance") composed of Tajiks. Non-Pashtun military-political groupings and regional leaders who had played a decisive role in the overthrow of the Taliban-Pashtun regime demanded a legal insurance of an adequate position in all power structures for their representatives. It was their milieu the persistent calls for a revival of Afghanistan in federative basis sounded from.

Pashtuns, in their turn, striving to reinstate their privileged position to a maximally possible extent were trying to retain a unitary slant of the state. Mutual divergences and mistrust continued to reign in the milieu of non-Pashtun leaders though they had the biggest armed formations at their disposal.

But Pashtuns are disconnected according to tribal, clan and territorial signs. Opposition was projected both towards the Interim Authority of Afghanistan whose power block was controlled mostly by non-Pashtuns, as for the economic one it was governed by the representatives of Pashtuns.

Another hot-button issue of nation-wide significance appeared the one of Islam status definition in state activities, correlation of Islam with secular standards. The westernized nationalistic wing of the Interim Authority of Afghanistan, including Hamid Karzai himself, had a stake in confining the functions of the clergy concerned with the governance over the state. Another part of the political establishment of Afghanistan which consisted mostly of "northern" votaries and field commanders of mujahideen (M. Fahim, Y. Qanuni, A. Dostum, Ismael Khan, K. Khalili and others) acted in favor of searching for a reasonable balance between Islamic and secular principles setting out from the positions of "nationalists-grounders". At the same time a considerable part of former mujahideen supported the point of view held by the leaders of clerical parties (B. Rabbani, A. Sayyaf) who stood for unconditional supremacy of Islamic norms between the adherents of Islamic and secular power unfolded around the Constitution of the country and in the course of subsequent general elections.

So, for the first time in the history of Afghanistan, the general elections of the President of the country were held in October 8, 2004. In defiance of expectations of the majority that great errors will be inherent in any new matter, notwithstanding the really admitted separate mistakes and omissions one can state that the elections passed relatively in a more democratic manner as compared with some states of Central Asia. 23 claimants were running for presidents; 18 persons being registered.

In the republics of Central Asia considered to be more developed as against Afghanistan only two or three persons are nominated at analogical elections. As for Turkmenistan there is one candidate in general.

The results of elections in Afghanistan not only astonished the world, but to some extent they are seen as edifying ones either. In the Islamic state of Afghanistan it was Hamid Karzai who became the President of the country, being Pashtun by nationality. Out of 99,9 % of votes 55,4 % were given to him. Other votes presented to his opponents were distributed in the following way: Yunis Qanuni, Tajik-16,3 %, Haji Mohammad Mohaqiq, Hazara-11%, Dostum, Uzbek-10 % [1].

Some political scientists account for such a democratic process as to the elections as follows: Karzai didn't enjoy all 100 % of votes because his power doesn't comprise all the provinces at a running, there are leaders of their own, for the time being different areas sustain dissociation (officially only about 10 % of the country's territory refers to non-submitting regions).

But the cause lies evidently much deeper. The formation of the common Afghan team of leadership was no last factor here: Vice-presidents of the country became Ahmad Zia Masood, brother of the deceased Ahmad Shah Masood, Tajik, and Khalili, Hazara, the post of Defense Vice-minister accrued to Uzbek General Rashid Dostum. There exists also the opinion that a part of Afghans who don't submit to the central power vindicated their votes by means of arms. But that fact is of importance that still they gave their votes having expressed their conscientious attitude to the fortune of the country and managed to influence it.

The position of the Tajiks of Afghanistan who were supposed to strongly vie with Karzai looked in reality as unclear and unstable. The group of Ahmad Shah Masood's brothers dissevered—one of them headed by Ahmad Zia Masood, Burhanuddin Rabbani's brother-in-law (being at the same time a leader of the group) supported Karzai. At the elections this group showed that it is useless to stand in opposition towards the Pashtun majority and that the pursuing of this streamline won't serve a further union of Afghanistan.

Another group of Ahmadali Masood with the disciple of his brother Ahmad Shah Masood, Yunis Qanuni (marshal Mohammad Fakhim being a group leader) demonstrated their non-resignation with the opinion of the Pashtun majority in the country and their intention to continue the struggle in favor of the Tajiks interests.

The cause of the inter-Tajik cleavage can be also accounted for by the interrelations between Burhanuddin Rabbani and Yunis Qanuni. It was a support of Karzai at Bonn Conference on the part of Qanuni that gave rise to all this. At that time when nominating for a head of the Interim Authority the candidatures of Karzai and Rabbani were considered; Qanuni, being the leader of United Front, supported the first one. Now Rabbani jointly with his brother-in-law took advantage of the opportunity to revenge on Qanuni.

But if to analyze the results of voting along the provinces with the prevailing Tajik population the above-mentioned version on revenge on the part of Rabbani aimed against Qanuni is not confirmed.

In the provinces mentioned Qanuni didn't manage to gain high percentage of votes like Karzai, Mohaqiq or Dostum did.

For example, in the provinces inhabited by Tajiks he enjoyed the following results:

Baghlan (39%), Samangan (38%), Ghor (46%), Parwan (57%), Kapisa (41%), Herat (34%), Badakhshan (40%), Balkh (26%), Badghis (31%), only in Panjshir, his native land, he got 95 % of votes.

In the provinces with Pashtun population Karzai obtained the following results: Fariyab (74 %), Nimroz (89 %), Helmand (90 %), in native land Kandahar (91 %).

Haji Mohammad Mohaqiq, being from Hazara, enjoyed a high percentage of votes in the provinces with Hazara population: Bamiyan (76 %), Daikondi (84 %). Dostum, being Uzbek, got 74 % of votes in Jowzjan (74 %) and Fariyab (72 %). What do the results enumerated testify to? May be, Tajiks are really democratic and impassionate. Or there confirmed Qanuni's predictions that due to falsifications and forges in regard to votes on the part of the central government and its accomplices he won't manage to gain high percentage. [2].

A relative democratic character of presidential elections in Afghanistan (as against analogical elections in Central Asian states) is proved by the fact that one of nominees for the top state post was a woman—Dr. Masuda Jalali.

In spite of separate drawbacks and omissions the presidential elections in Afghanistan upon the whole evidence to the demonstration of tolerance and national consent, promotion to peace, they inspired hope for a bright future with the people sustaining sufferings.

Thus, the President of the country is a head of the Afghan state, his powers comprise all the bodies under state auspices without exception his executive authorities embrace the activities performed by the Council of Ministers. Thus, in accordance with the Fundamental Law of IRA a decisive role in the system of supreme state authorities belongs to the President of the country who as its head effectuates all his legislative, executive and judicial authorities in conformity with the Constitution and the Laws of Afghanistan. Evidently, when investing the President with unrestrained power the authors of the Constitution proceeded from the extremely complicated realities concerned with the post-conflict situation in the country which had been enduring the war in the course of 25 years.

The matters of priority for the new administration were those of profound reforms in reference to the public authority in the centre and in provinces.

At present the general staff of state officials consists of about 300 thousand people. Alongside with the initially formed 29 Ministries in pursuance with Bonn Agreement the state structure accreted with numerous committees and commissions frequently duplicating the activities of the bodies of an analogical orientation.

Maintenance of the bureaucratic machinery is a heavy burden for the state budget of the country assigned for a fiscal year (since March 21) in the amount of 550 million US dollars under the deficiency in 350 million US dollars (supposed to be covered at the expense of foreign aid).

An administrative chaos opens a wide space for corruption, orders of seniority and nepotism putting barriers on the ways of the country's development. The government vainly tries to cardinally diminish the state machinery, optimize its structure and curb corruption. Into the bargain, one should pay attention to the fact that not infrequently local authorities, field commanders, first of all, don't transfer obtained revenues, from customs in particular, to the centre. In this interview to "Armani-e Milliy" paper Hamid Karzai notes the facts when the authorities of separate provinces didn't transfer taxes to the centre. At the meetings with the governors of 12 provinces which had outstanding debts in the amount over 400 million dollars owned to the national treasury he declared that in case the situation does not improve the government won't be able to work with a good efficacy.

The state administration of Afghanistan is well conscious of the urgency of the problem concerned with an efficiency of public administration through a systemic reform and a validation of its fundamental grounds in the Constitution of the country.

In September 8, 2005 parliamentary elections took place in the country. First of all, one ought to scrutinize how a pre-election combat for deputy mandates into the superior legislative body of the country deployed.

As per the clause 36 of the ISA Fundamental Law ere long before the elections into the parliament and local councils (shuros) there started a struggle for the places into the superior body of the country and its local legislative bodies.

The legislation of the country doesn't restrict to nomination of civilians. All in all on the eve of the elections 5800 persons ran for deputies, but there were only 400 places for claimants [3]. These were representatives of various ethnic, clan-tribal, age and professional groups of male and female parts of population, provinces. Even former top functionaries of Taliban registered themselves as candidates.

> Mavlavi Muttavakil—former Minister of Foreign Affairs;
> Mullah Hakiyar—former Minister of State Security;
> Mavlavi Mahmadhasan—Vice Prime Minister of Rabbani's government;
> Mavlavi Abdurazzak—former Minister of Interior;
> Mavlavi Muttaki—former Minister of Culture;
> Mullah Ubaidulla—former Minister of Defense.

The nomination and all pre-elective organizational-propagandistic campaign were conducted according to the regulations of the Central Election Committee and the Fundamental Law of the country.

Equal conditions were established for each candidate in order they might organize meetings with their constituency, explicate their pre-elective program. Each candidate was bound to be granted with an air time free of charge—five minutes on radio and four minutes on TV.

But equal rights were not ensured with equal availabilities. So, Mass Media consisting of 76 state-owned and private radio and television channels and over 130 newspapers are focused mainly in Kabul as a capital and around it. The population of the country where only 28 % can read and write and the rest part is illiterate lacked information about the nominees to the Parliament and local authority, their political platform. The illiterate population of remote provinces had no idea about the rules and orders of voting, their rights, availability of arguments, how to ask candidates about common national interests, whether the formers are able to solve acute social and economic problems of the country. Common people displayed no interest in narrowly mercantile, clan and party considerations of the nominees. The people wished to take advantage of the opportunity in order to nominate genuine patriots, honest citizens with unblemished reputation into the superior legislative body of the country. But deputy chairs were needed by corrupted officials, armed militants, leaders of extremist groups in order to go on with criminal antinational deeds under the guise of deputy immunity. And it stands to reason that these categories of well-to-do citizens enjoyed greater availabilities for gaining elections. Just that predetermined an acuteness of pre-elective struggle in the country. Criminogenic atmosphere was highly tense. There was no day when about 50-60 people wouldn't perish because of terrorist acts in Kabul, Kandahar, Zabul and other provinces. Among them there were American military officers, journalists and activists, members of election committees, nominees for deputies. Into the bargain, only for ensuring of the very polls the state meted over 60 thousand military men from the troops of the Ministry of Interior. Reactionary forces, Al-Qaida militants killed everyone who supported the acting government and its orders. The tensest atmosphere reigned in Kabul and in the South of the country. In Kandahar they murdered Mullah Abdullah Malang.

Hamid Karzai who pursues an ambiguous policy in reference to Taliban during the visit of Pakistani Prime Minister to Kabul in July 2005 was compelled to evince discontent with frequent penetration of terrorists from Pakistan to Afghanistan. But as for the latter, their number in Afghanistan itself is great enough. These are separate militants from the detachments of Taliban and Al-Qaida whom Hamid Karzai tried to integrate into the Afghan society under the slogan of national reconciliation. In January 10, 2006 he addressed the leader of Taliban Mullah Umar to return to the country and to pour into its life.

The public opinion poll among civilians of Afghanistan and the Afghans residing abroad brought to light the opinion of electors; the items included asked what is to conduct proper elections and what is to be expected from nominees; the future voters demonstrated their doubts referring to the illiteracy of 72 % of the population because this category of people can hardly analyze conscientiously the situation concerned with elections of deputies, they are unable to argue, to put proper questions; not all provinces enjoy the availabilities to the listen to the radio, to watch TV, to read newspapers which merely don't reach their regions. Many people even don't understand the essence and importance of the parliament. Electors have no regulations related to the rules of organization of elections, pre-elective programs of candidates. The majority of respondents were mindful of inducement on the part of authorities non-admissible in the course of a pre-elective campaign according to the rules; they remarked that officials may avail of their official position. People wanted to see worthy individuals elected by the nation, those who wouldn't pursue their mercantile interests but would care of the benefit of their common compatriots. They suggested that in case of lodged complaints dwelling on the behavior of candidates to the Central Executive Committee (CEC) and a confirmation of expounded accusations one should observe a principal approach in reference to offenders. One ought not to admit the nominees breaking the rules of propagation of themselves and the programs of their own when 48 hours remain before polls.

The suggested that drug criminals, former militants who had committed crimes in the past, were not admitted to the parliament.

The questionnaire manifested that the public opinion formed among the population about mujahideen regarded the latter as the force defending the national interests of the country [4].

In the course of pre-elective campaign a lot of organizational errors and blunders were made. In a number of provinces, e.g. in Kandahar and Jalalabad, the polls were not free and just. In Baghlan province 12 settlements were included into one electoral center without an agreement with the local population.

The European Union whose 120 representatives observed over the process of preparation for the elections expressed anxiety as to the atmosphere in a number of provinces when instead of individual voting people threw packs of the bulletins into urns, i.e. threats, frightening and pressure upon electors had been used.

Thus, in September 18 in Afghanistan after 36 years of interruption there were held elections into the lower chamber of the Parliament (Wolesi Jirga) and provincial councils; in October 24—in 40 days expired after the polls—their results were counted.

They terminated a recurrent stage of the establishment of the lawful power in the country preconditioned by Bonn Agreements of 2001 [5].

There were 5800 claimants who challenged for 488 parliamentary chairs. The preparation for the elections and their organization cost 159 million dollars.

But in view of the tense military-political atmosphere, deficiency of finances, technical and organizational non-readiness the elections had been postponed several times and it told negatively upon voters' attendance. If the attendance of the presidential elections of 2004 was equal to 80 per cent, at the parliamentary polls it reduced to 50 per cent, though this indicator is of no principal importance, since the Law doesn't establish a low threshold of voter's attendance. It doesn't speak about the moods in the society.

The present elections took place in the surroundings when the period of pink hopes caused by intensive dissipation of Taliban by the Northern Alliance and coalitional forces had already passed, but no notable changes in the economic plight of population could be observed.

International aid doesn't come in time, it is not disinterested, the major part of it settles in the pockets of foreign task-managers, international auditors and advisers, it is spent for office leasing, it is wasted for bribes given under registration of NGOs international aid is spread through, going counter to Hamid Karzai's wish who wanted it to enter directly to the government. As corruption permeates all Afghan society that one who was rich becomes much richer. Poor people have been dragging out a miserable existence. The public opinion poll undertaken for clearing out public opinion in the course of preparation for elections showed that the population doesn't believe that their votes may be of any significance. People rightly foretold that in the Parliament there will sit the representatives of mujahideen and those who had been assigned for the role of "puppeteers" in advance.

Being aware of the Law on elections enabling to nominate members from parties and political movements on the eve of the elections those wishing to run for deputies united in 80 various parties. So, there was nothing astonishing in their leaders declaring one type statement.

The results of the polls demonstrate the following apportionment of political forces:

50 %—former mujahideen; 25 %—adherents of democratic views; 12-15 %—those who support the government; 5 %—former members of NDPA; 5 %—representatives of Taliban movement. The Parliament stood in opposition to the government because 130 senators out of 249 from the Lower

Chamber (Wolesi Jirga) could not be suspected of sympathies towards the government. 25 % of parliamentary places were occupied by women.

Mujahideen making up a half of deputies present the following apportionment of political forces and groups:

52 places—members of Islamic Unity Party of Afghanistan (B. Rabbani);

18 places—Islamic Party of Afghanistan (Y. Hekmatyar);

17 places—members of the National Islamic Movement of Afghanistan (Abdul Rashid Dostum);

16 places—members of the Islamic Unity Party of the People of Afghanistan (Haji Mohammad Mohaqiq);

15 places—members of the People's Democratic Party of Afghanistan (Khalq (Masses) faction and 5 Parcham (Banner) faction members);

9 places—members of the Islamic Union for the Liberation of Afghanistan (Abdul Rabb al-Rasul Sayyaf);

8 places—members of the National Islamic Front of Afghanistan (Sayyed Ahmad Gailani);

7 places—members of Afghan Mellat movement (Anwar al-Haq Ahadi);

2 places—disciples of Zahir Shah;

2 places—not being in any parties—disciples of Hamid Karzai.

Per one place: the National Solidarity Party of Afghanistan (Sayyed Mansur Nadiri) and Jamoati davoi vakhobiya; Youth Solidarity Party of Afghanistan (Jamil Karzai, an American immigrant, militant from Herat). In the new parliament deputies are mentioned in the context of their former party affiliation. So, Yunis Qanuni, Chairman of the New Afghanistan Party is spoken of as a member of the Islamic Society of Afghanistan.

Formation of associations and factions in the parliament depends on coincidence of the interests of ethnic groups. As for ethnic balance in Wolesi Jirga it looks like this: Pashtun—111, Tajik—69, Hazara—26, Uzbek—20, Turkmen and Arab—4 each, per two and per one representatives—from each national minority.

Dari-speaking parliamentarians constitute the majority of 135 persons. These are Tajiks, Uzbeks, Turkmens, Arabs, Kizilbashis and others. Pashto-speaking—114, namely: Pashtuns, Pashai, Nuristani, Beluji. State languages in pursuance with the Constitution are Pashto and Dari. But sometimes problems are arising, since Tajiks, Uzbeks and Turkmens don't master Pashto. It can cause problems in work of the parliament. One can suppose that in the period when not Party interests are insured, but the rights of nationalities are observed; ethnic minorities and certain layers of society being implied.

The failure of actually merited, progressive people of Afghanistan at the elections can be accounted for by the government's disability to defend the really worthy popular nominees. The results of the elections manifested acute political, clan, national-ethnic contradictions taking place in the society.

The acuteness of the pre-elective struggle is evidenced by the facts of physical reprisals in reference to candidates. According to the Afghan Law if a member of the parliament falls ill, leaves for another place or loses capability of functioning he is replaced by the candidate following him in close vote. But into what can it eventuate in the country overfilled with arms, where every male is resolute, proud and independent?

50 officers included into election committees were accused of gerrymandering, sale of voters' identification cards, substitution of bulletins; the latter being issued in the amount of 40 million exceeding considerably the number of real voters.

The organizers themselves were dissatisfied with the results of the elections. Just after the elections Kabul was visited by Condoleezza Rice, State Secretary of the USA, Rumsfeld, the Minister of Defense and Zalmai Khalilzai, former US Ambassador in Afghanistan (working now in Iraq), who arrived in October 23, 2005. The reason of Washington activeness lies in non-consolatory results of the elections and weakened positions of the USA protégés. Evidently they are alarmed being afraid of the new parliament which probably may prohibit the persons with dual citizenship to occupy high posts. Minister of Interior Jalali has already resigned. Wardak, Minister of Defense, and Ahadi, Minister of Finance are in a shaky position.

For these reasons Carina Pereli, expert in UN monitoring over the polls in Afghanistan, might have been dismissed.

Hamid Karzai himself, having lost the support of the majority in the new parliament being aware of political moods of his opponents not having achieved economic sponsorship of his patrons begins to be behaving in a detached manner. He demands that coalitional forces made preliminary agreements on military operations, he insists on extermination of "the nests of terrorism" in the countries of their preparation, but not in Afghanistan, refuses from the transoceanic guard, condemns the actions of American "special propagandists" who in a scoffing manner burned publicly the bodies of two killed Afghans, declared to be Talibs; that goes counter to the religion and traditions of Moslems.

Thus, the newly elected parliament crowns the effectuation of all the items of Bonn Conference held in 2001. There formed an internal political system in Afghanistan. At the first session of the new Parliament in December 19, 2005 in the difficult combat with such leaders of Islamic society of Afghanistan as B. Rabbani (Islamic Society of Afghanistan), Mohaqiq (Islamic Unity Party of the People of Afghanistan), Rasul Sayyaf (Islamic Union of Liberation of Afghanistan), Sayyed Gailani (National Islamic Front of Afghanistan), Ulumi (National Unity Party)—it was Mohammad Yunis Qanuni, a leader of the United National and Islamic Front for the Salvation of Afghanistan (UNIFSA) who had united 13 various political parties and movements, whom they elected as a speaker. The representatives of the mentioned front occupy the major part of places in the Parliament [6].

Notes:

1. Vishal Chandra "Afghan Election: From Here to Where?" Asianaffairs, November 2004, p. 11
2. "Ruzi Nav", February 4, 2004. No. 33
3. BBC broadcast dated August 19, 2005
4. ibidem
5. Pre-elective Situation in Afghanistan
6. "Asia-Plus" Newspaper dated December 21, 2005.

CHAPTER 3

Contemporary Economic Situation of the Islamic Republic of Afghanistan, Prospects of Its Revival

After the withdrawal of the Soviet troops from Afghanistan in 1989 the forces of different parties and alliances with diverse ideologies assumed the governance, but none of them was able to put an end to the war and to ensure peace in the country. Due to non-availability of human resources, specialists competent in management, owing to ethnic contradictions, extremist and politicized tendencies the government turned to be unable to stabilize the political situation and normalize the social and economic life in the country.

In spite of tangible progresses of the international community on resurgence of relative peace and stability in Afghanistan the country has been meanwhile confronting grave problems.

Old reference-points and values based on the principles of feudal relations, clan-tribal, ethnic, linguistic, religious and gender priorities were subject to extermination.

It is important to take into account that if in practice the obligations of the international community on rendering aid to Afghanistan are not fulfilled, if proper economic and financial investments are not deposited, nothing would guarantee that Afghanistan won't return to the bitter times of the civil war.

In order to achieve peace and stability in Afghanistan it is necessary, first of all, to restore the economy of this country.

According to Bonn Agreement the primary goal alongside with establishment of peace and security, creation of state power foundations was aimed at reinstatement of economic infrastructure as well; the latter being realized very poorly in practice. As official Afghan persons declared, in order to restore the country 20 billion dollars were needed for the first five years. But for the initial two years out of 4,7 billion dollars promised by the international community the latter procured only 1.3 billion.

In the framework of the resolution passed by Tokyo International Conference on the assistance in public and economic resurgence of Afghanistan (February, 2002) on allotment of 4.5 billion dollars in 2002 almost 2 billion dollars were sent to the country being referred by UNO and nonprofit organizations.

Out of achievements related to this program one can mention obtaining of foreign aid and completion of obligations of the countries-donors. Taking into consideration a humanitarian character of a part of these assistance activities and an enormous volume of destructions one can account for imperceptible outcomes concerned with the sums expected, which aren't seen conspicuously up to the present moment.

It is caused by a number of reasons. Firstly, the great bulk of those resources was disbursed not for the development projects, but to cover humanitarian needs.

Secondly, the cumber of the mechanism related to the financial aid referred through the channels of UNO and NGOs turned out to be a new area difficult for being dealt with, not infrequent duplication of UNO and NGOs activities results in reduction of efficacy concerned with external investments. Alongside with it many states-donors prefer to refer financial aid through the national NGOs of their own that doesn't promote development of multilateral cooperation.

Restoration of the economy of Afghanistan can be achieved both by internal and external endeavors, using both internal ad external potentials international community being implied.

In this third chapter the author dwells on the issues in separate paragraphs: "The Position and Prospects of Intergovernmental Economic Cooperation between the Republic of Tajikistan and the Islamic State of Afghanistan" and "The Problems of Cooperation between Central Asian States and Afghanistan".

PARAGRAPH 1

History and Contemporary Status of Intergovernmental Economic Cooperation between the Republic of Tajikistan and the Islamic Republic of Afghanistan

The economic cooperation between Tajikistan and Afghanistan had been forming historically being complicated and ambiguous. It consists relatively of two periods: the Soviet one when Tajikistan carried out the economic ties with this country through all-Union framework, and the period after gaining independence (from 1991 up to nowadays).

In April 1980 following the changes introduced in the politics of Afghanistan the Revolutionary Council in imitation to socialist states introduced article 4 into "The Basic Principles of the Democratic Republic of Afghanistan" running that " . . . The People's Democratic Party of Afghanistan is a leading and guiding force of society" [1].

In both countries party guidance over national economy was effectuated in one and the same manner and this enabled the Afghan leadership to domesticate an experience and methods of economical activity from Central Asian republics, including neighboring Tajikistan.

According to the Treaty of Friendship, Cooperation and Good Neighborliness between the USSR and the Republic of Afghanistan dated December 5, 1978 there was developed the program of cultural and scientific cooperation between the USSR, its subjects and the Republic of Afghanistan that envisaged rendering of aid to this country for development of different spheres.

In the enactment of Politburo of the Central Committee CPSU "On Our Steps Concerned with the Development of Conditions around Afghanistan" adopted in December 1979 it was particularly noted that "carrying out the measures specified the Politburo took into account the strategic plight of Afghanistan. The

Afghan state is in immediate closeness with our frontiers being the neighbor of Central Asian republics. Therefore it is important to trouble about the security of our socialist motherland" [2].

It is worth mentioning that the conditions and standards of development of the two states, the forms of political power and administration, productive forces, level of their development, per capita power consumption, availability of infrastructure, qualification of specialists, the nature of economy specialization in Tajikistan and Afghanistan were not only different but non-incommensurable either.

If the economy of the Tajik SSR was regulated from the center, in Afghanistan it was mostly in a competence of private owners.

The analysis of the achievements obtained according to the eleventh five-year plan gives an assessment to initial economic availabilities of Tajikistan for cooperation with other states, including Afghanistan.

The national revenue for 1981-1985 augmented for 14 per cent. As of July 1, 1985 there functioned 1236 sets of mechanized and automated production lines and 356 units of equipment with programmed control in the industry of the republic.

For the fiver years over 130 manufactured denominations of goods were put out in the system of production. The industrial output increased for 21 per cent, its cost exceeded to one belonging to the tenth five-year plan for 4.6 billion rubles.

The branches determining technical progress developed in outstripping tempos, here refer: power engineering, mechanical engineering and metal processing, sewing, chemical, petrochemical and mining industries.

In this period Afghanistan finding itself in the surroundings of the perennial wars pursued the economic policy based on mixed economy providing wide opportunities to national entrepreneurs and foreign capital.

The analysis and confrontation of economic indicators of the two countries within the mentioned historic period show that if in Tajikistan the whole output volume befalls the share of the state, in Afghanistan the private sector of craftsmanship put out over 40 per cent of the gross industrial output. At this time the domestic market in Afghanistan needed extension. Wide-scaled production was unable to satisfy it in a brief space of time. Under these conditions the government decided to augment commodity output and saturate the market by means of accelerated development of artisan production.

In particular, according to the main streamlines of economic and social development for 1987-1991 they envisaged to augment gross production output in the artisan sector for 14,9 per cent within the specified period [3].

This accelerated development of artisan production and the one concentrated at private factories required financing or external investing.

And here it was the USSR that came to succor. The strategy of foreign policy ties of the USSR with Afghanistan within the period of 1986-1990 proceeded from the resolutions of the 27th Congress of the CPSU a sequence of which runs as follows: "First of all, economic interaction with socialist sister nations needs to be improved and enriched and the cooperation with developing countries should be intensified to the utmost" [4].

The Soviet-Afghan Treaty of January 16, 1987 (all Soviet republics taking part in its realization, *author's note*) envisaged multilateral aid to Afghanistan in industry, agriculture, construction industry and frontier trade in Northern provinces.

In early 1987 the Afghan side invoked the USSR to render assistance in launching of industrial and some other objects. It is common knowledge that the objects built and exploited with assistance of the USSR provided nearly 45 per cent of state budget revenues at the expense of inner sources [5].

The expenditures concerned with gratis aid were formed with the participation of all union republics, including Tajik SSR.

As the Afghan conflict had been developing and the internal political situation in this country had been accruing its negative force, fulfillment of the obligations on construction of the mentioned objects taken by the Soviet Union and its subjects endured hampering.

The products exported from Tajikistan to Afghanistan consisted of hydraulics, cables, spare parts for automobiles, chemical fertilizers, electric power and commercial machine-building products. In the period of national reconciliation patronage and frontier ties served for further deepening of Soviet-Afghan friendship. The adjustment of these ties was to the liking of oppositional forces as it conduced to the strengthening of coalitional governance; the factor being of additional importance.

The Republic of Tajikistan, being a Soviet republic yet, since 1985 advanced as an initiator of patronage ties between Gorno-Badakhshan Autonomous Region, Kurgan-Tube and Kulob regions of Tajikistan and Badakhshan, Balkh, Takhar and Kunduz provinces of the Republic of Afghanistan, which opened new availabilities and perspectives in the relations between the neighboring countries.

Taking into consideration the plight of Afghanistan the economy of which was completely destroyed by the war these patronage ties bore a character of unilateral gratis aid on the part of Tajikistan for the benefit of the neighboring provinces of Afghanistan. Thus, the volume of aid for 1988-1989 totaled 3,9 million rubles and that are referred by the ministries and departments averaged 3,7 million rubles [6]

The Tajik SSR State Planning Committee meted out additional commodities (Appendix 1) the regions patronizing the neighboring provinces for their further delivery to Afghanistan.

Gradually the patronage ties in the terms of unilateral aid began transforming into direct connections of the two states acquiring a character of legal agreements. What were the potentialities of Tajikistan for the given period?

The Republic of Tajikistan was on the eve of the USSR collapse when economic ties between the subjects of the Soviet Union started to disintegrate.

The research of Tajikistan economy on the verge of its transference to market relations shows that by the year 1980 the import of goods exceeded their export for the amount of one billion one hundred million rubles. Already since 1990 as against 1980 national revenue reduced for 1,2 %. Labor productivity decreased for 1,6 % [7]. The projected task concerned with the gross output of agricultural produce for 1989 was fulfilled for 82 % [ibidem p.8].

Under the setback in production marked at the end of the eleventh five-year plan high tempos of natality couldn't have told upon living standard. Thus, over the years 1986-1987 manpower resources of the republic increased at the expense of the youth entering their able-bodied age for 129,2 thousand people, but the transference of outfits on self-accounting and self-financing basis, applying of new labor remuneration conditions eventuated into a release of non-demanded labor force.

In 1987 only 64,3 per cent of labor resources were engaged in the social production of the republic [9].

Having at its disposal rich labor, energetic, mineral raw stuff resources, potential of experts, machine-building complex, mining and extractive industries, diversified agriculture Tajikistan which found itself in the surroundings of the disintegrated USSR confronted the urgency of searching for the ways of integration and the cooperation both with CIS countries and other states of far and near abroad.

There are favorable opportunities for cooperation with Afghanistan having similar geographic and climatic conditions, common water resources when both countries have enormous labor force; hereby Tajikistan has auto and railway lines, ferries and now into the bargain they are constructing bridges and prolonging transnational roads.

Afghanistan being in the conditions of enduring war needs the assistance from outside, since all the branches of its economy have been sustaining the deep protracted slump. The production of all items of goods as against the year 1978 reduced almost for 20 per cent. In 1991 the state budget deficiency constituted 71 per cent in reference to its outlay part. The outstanding foreign debts of Afghanistan averaged 7.8 billion US dollars to that time; nearly 92 per cent—US$ 7.2 billion befalling the share of the USSR.

The analysis of the state and the tendency of agricultural development for the recent 13 years (1972-1985) displays a considerable reduction in agricultural production, including wheat—for 40 per cent, grapes—for 20 per cent, cotton—more than three times; wool—two times less, rawstock—for 40 per cent. Wheat production in 1988 diminished as against 1983 for 5 per cent [10].

The research of the agriculture of that period proved that Afghan farmers making up 90 per cent of the country's population were unable to properly cope with farm operations. For example, in Mazar-i-Sharif and Kattagan provinces harvest losses amounted to the half of the sprouted crops in totality [11].

Out of over 400 industrial enterprises a considerable part of which befalls state and mixed sectors the greater part is either in the state of standing idle or it operates in partial capacity owing to the lack of electric power, fuel, raw stuffs, qualified human resources.

Natural gas production as against 1978 reduced twelve times, coal—for 40 per cent, cement—for 30 per cent, cotton—6 times less, cotton wares—4 times less [12].

After the withdrawal of the Soviet troops from Afghanistan when they got down to implementing of the national reconciliation course the economic policy of the Afghan government started to change.

In the enactment of Central Committee of the CPSU Politburo dated January 24, 1989 "On the Measures in Reference to Forthcoming Withdrawal of Soviet Troops from Afghanistan" the following sequence runs: "Afghan comrades express their comprehension as to the issue of withdrawal of Soviet troops having been resolved . . . , but at the same time estimating the situation soundly they mark that they won't do without Soviet aid completely. In their opinion, this aid might be rendered in other forms differing from the current ones . . . [13].

In the new situation Najibullah's regime started to reorient the wide-scale multilateral ties of Afghanistan with the USSR to regional economic cooperation; the republics of Central Asia being in consideration of priority.

Due to its geographic closeness and a comparably developed economy of that time Tajikistan might have played a certain role in adjustment of economic ties with Afghanistan. The leadership of the Republic of Afghanistan hoped to use this factor reckoning that Central Asian state, including Tajikistan, would be a source of catering for the urgent needs of the country in power carriers, several items of food stuffs and industrial goods; CIS countries having stopped their delivery. So, at the first all-Afghan Congress of artisans it was articulated that "the aid of the USSR in the framework of the agreement on direct ties between Afghanistan and separate regions of the Soviet Union will be attracted for supporting craftsmanship" [14]. In October 27, 1990 bilateral agreement was signed in Tashkent on the main streamlines of cooperation in the framework of direct ties for 1991-1992 between the Tajik SSR and Afghanistan.

Taking into account the fact that under the conditions of dry climate in the northern provinces of Afghanistan irrigation and melioration were of vital importance experts and workers of Tajikistan jointly with their Soviet colleagues took part in the implementation of the projects on construction of 23 artesian wells and 115 shaft wells.

Tajik geologists, water conservation experts rendered assistance to Afghan organizations dealing with a construction of hydraulic works; they have designed the schemes of land utilization in Northern Afghanistan. The measures pursued enabled to extend the square of watered pastures for 600 thousand hectares. In its turn this promoted to improvement of living conditions for nomad stock-breeders.

Since 1979 Tajik experts included into the Soviet brigades rendered assistance to Afghanistan in launching of 5 engineering stations, 3 soil-agrochemical laboratories, seed-control laboratories on cereal crops, stations for artificial insemination of animals [15].

State factory-farm enterprise of the Tajik SSR in the framework of technical assistance for the period of 1986-1989 referred various technique, equipment, spare parts, seeds, veterinary medications to Afghanistan on a gratis basis; the sum of the items listed having amounted to 5551.6 thousand rubles.

To render assistance in the combat with locusts in 1986-1989 annually 12 experts—agronomists-entomologists, agronomists—seed-growers and veterinarians—were sent to the Republic of Afghanistan for 60 days [16].

Afghanistan government of those times passed a resolution in 1991 on allocating 50 thousand hectares of land in Khushtepa area of Kunduz province for "Aftoj" joint Afghan-Tajik venture.

Currently due to limitations in regard to the exported production it is non-expedient to extend the lands laid under grain in Tajikistan at the expense of reducing raw cotton production.

In the sphere of grain production cooperation with neighboring Afghanistan is possible. There are the issues that were laid as the grounds of negotiations and the agreement between the former Minister of grain products of Tajikistan Abdullojanov and the Afghan entrepreneur Gulyam Hazrat Ibragim; the event having taken place in Dushanbe in 1991.

Unification of the experts' efforts in cotton-growing, light and food industries of Tajikistan with Afghan colleagues through the reclamation of the Northern lands of Afghanistan—irrigation of dry areas, selection of cotton with its further processing—are of prospective significance for the both countries.

For the period of 1980-1990 the rate of all types of fuel production in Tajikistan reduced and in reference to the level of 1980 they engendered the following indicators respectively: petroleum—36,8 per cent, coal—57 per cent; gas—50 per cent.

Thereby annually Tajikistan imports all types of fuel from other CIS states in the volume of 240 million dollars (by conversion to foreign currency). The primary importers are Uzbekistan and Turkmenistan.

Forecasting of the situation for the nearest future gives no warranty for optimistic moods in regard to the mentioned countries setting up close economy ties with the countries of the East and Europe and having a stake in transformation of their raw stuff resources into hard currency. For example,

Turkmenistan having entered into agreement with Afghanistan according to which main gas pipeline of a long diameter will be laid intends to export gas to Pakistan and other oriental states through the territory of the given country.

Taking into account the growing demands for Turkmenistan gas on the part of Far and Near abroad Turkmens and Uzbeks deliver their gas to Tajikistan at world prices of the international market.

The closeness of Tajikistan and Afghanistan enables to make commercial transactions on gas with the lowest costs.

There shapes the situation when Afghanistan reckons for catering of its needs in electric power and Tajikistan needs Afghan gas.

Under the circumstances when both countries are confined in currency reserves (and for Afghanistan gas remains the main article of currency earnings into the budget) the option befalls an exchange dealing with exchange value of gas and electric power on mutually acceptable basis. In so far as this issue is concerned yet since 1992 the Tajik-Afghan negotiations have commenced; the start being given by the visit of Abdul Samad Salah, Minister of Industry and Mining Affairs, to Tajikistan. At that time the parties came to the conclusion that the following transaction is possible in cooperation in this branch: —Exchange of Afghan gas for delivery of electric power from Tajikistan. In the period indicated the Tajik party offered the price of 8 cents per 1 kW/h. Afghans regarded this price as too high (for comparison—the level of prices in separate countries of Asian region per kW/h averaged: in Laos—3,05, India—3,8, Pakistan—3,8, Indonesia—5,3, Singapore—6,7 dollars). When entering the agreement on mutual deliveries of Afghan gas to Tajikistan and Tajik electric power to Afghanistan and to settling mutual accounts on the results of the year ended it was decided make deliveries according to actual volumes of outlays. As for the variation in prices (gas is more expensive than electricity) Tajikistan was liable to reimburse it either by hard currency or by compensations in the terms of goods and food stuffs of local production delivered to Afghanistan; aluminum and chinaware being implied in the inventory. To address these issues in March 1992 the Tajik delegation visited Kabul, it consisted of the representatives from Goskomgaz (State Committee for gas affairs), Ministry of External Economic Links and Ministry of Finance. Respective protocols had been signed. At that time there were signed tens of contracts jointly with Afghan entrepreneurs on building bakeries, confectionery factories, enterprises specializing in biscuits and all sorts of sweets, as well as salt refineries and other objects.

Wide availabilities for recovery of Tajik economy under the circumstances of transition to market were opened by the Law "On Foreign Investments" adopted by the Supreme Soviet of Tajikistan dated March 14, 1992. According to this Law foreign investors are entitled to launch both joint ventures and own enterprises within the republic; they may take up shares and other securities, to participate in privatization of enterprises disowned by the state. The law ensures guarantees for foreign investitures.

In 1991 the Afghan Council of Ministers Office for direct foreign economic links directed the team of entrepreneurs for making contracts with "Tajikpotrebsoyuz" (Tajik Customers Association), "Tajikvneshtorg" (Tajik Foreign Trade), Ministry of Commerce, Ministry of Agriculture, Ministry of Light Industry and others. This trip was aimed at investment of the stock belonging to Afghan entrepreneurs into establishment of joint ventures for manufacturing of finished commodity.

Thus, in 1992 out of 80 joint ventures registered by the Ministry of external economic links 43 were Tajik-Afghan ventures. 109 commercial shops and the market "Afghan-Bazaar" were opened in that period in Tajikistan.

The amount of yearly earnings alone from customs duties paid by the joint Tajik-Afghan ventures made up 15 million rubles.

The agro-commercial cooperative firm "Tajikistan" proceeded to establishment of a number of joint Tajik-Afghan ventures in Dushanbe city, Kurgan-Tyube and Kanibadam towns to produce footwear, fabrics and leather working.

The Tajik-Afghan company "Afghan, Bukhara Co. Ltd" in addition to selling hand-woven carpet wares in Tajikistan tackled a very useful business—they opened a class-school in Dushanbe to train local girls and boys on the ancient craftsmanship of handmade carpet weaving. 22 young people of the capital had been mastering the secrets of the ancient trade in Mr. Bodghizi's workshops being taught by Afghan craftsmen.

Unfortunately, realization of the agreements achieved with Afghanistan was impeded first by the subversion of Najibullah's regime. Then by the assumption of power by mujahideen followed by the Taliban movement in Afghanistan which unleashed the bloody war in this country; into the bargain, the civil war broke out in Tajikistan itself.

Thus, in the field of external economic links under the declarations stated by Sigbatullah Mojadeddi, Chairman of Jihad Council and leader of the interim Islamic government of Afghanistan, certain anticipated reorientations have followed—first of all, stirring up of commercial and economic cooperation with those countries which rendered political, military, financial aid during Jihad: Pakistan and Iran, Saudi Arabia, Egypt, as well as the USA and other Western countries.

At the same time it can be presumed that the new government was ready to preserve and develop good relations with neighboring countries too. It stood to reason that a lot of urgent problems concerned with a post-war restoration of Afghanistan depended to a certain extent on cooperation with neighboring countries, here refer: liquidation of famine, agricultural development, employment, development of light and processing industries, transport, restoration of destroyed objects and many other activities of priority.

After relative neutralization of Taliban, establishment of peace on the Afghan earth, achievement of consent between hostile political groups, establishment of coalitional government, strengthening of state foundations, establishment of diplomatic relations with neighboring states there new availabilities have emerged for close fruitful cooperation between the Republic of Tajikistan and the Islamic Republic of Afghanistan.

They started to pay more attention to the issues in regard to social and economic relations with Afghanistan after the Republic of Tajikistan had gained independence.

The objectives pursued were: to stabilize political and economic situation in the neighboring state, to reduce terrorism, to preclude penetration of drugs into our country.

It is known that Tajikistan has been located in a cul-de-sac of the post-Soviet space geographically. And from this point of view stabilization of political, social and economic atmosphere in Afghanistan might be the basis for solving of the mentioned objective, since the Islamic Republic of Afghanistan enjoys an important geopolitical location being the core of Asia.

Therefore this region is in the focus of interests of the big world states for a long period of time. They are targeted to strengthen their sway in the Asian region. Moreover, Afghanistan is rich with natural resources and raw stuffs, i.e. this region has a rich economic potential.

Unfortunately, the enduring war in this country brought its social and economic plight to decay. The economy of the country, i.e. industry, agriculture, social sphere, infrastructure, communications—all this was completely destroyed.

In addition, for the period of Taliban governance the country converted into the testing-ground for the drives of international terrorism and religious extremism; the place of drugs production and trafficking being a threat not only for the region, but for the entire world either.

The experience of settling political conflicts proves that without necessary economic measures being ensured political resolutions lose their force. It is confirmed by the experience of stabilization in reference to the political atmosphere in Tajikistan.

It is worth mentioning that under the present circumstances there formed a favorable situation in the region for rendering aid to the Afghan people in the region cause of the nation's return to peaceful creative life, to participation in international cooperation.

Every progressive state should help the suffering Afghan people and inspire hope in it for getting back to the better future. The Tajik people is an equally concerned party, since the stabilization of political, economic and social situation in Afghanistan is a guarantee of the stability in the region Tajikistan is included into.

In this regard, the Republic of Tajikistan takes all actions to take an active part in the post-conflict reinstatement of Afghanistan. At that this good deed will also respond to economic interests of Tajikistan itself, as there may rise an opportunity of utilizing an economic potential of the projects on restoration of Afghanistan sponsored by international financial organizations and donors.

The new page of cooperation our nations opened in 1992 when diplomatic relations were established between the Republic of Tajikistan and the Islamic State of Afghanistan. The meetings of the leaders of the two countries in the terms of state visits become regular being aimed at concluding and implementation of intergovernmental agreements and organizing of legal consulting. In the course of visits the issues related to diversified, mutually beneficial cooperation between the two states are being discussed.

One should mention the role of Resolution No. 49 passed by the Government of the Republic of Tajikistan dated 5 February 2003 dwelling on creating of Tajik part of the intergovernmental commission of the Republic of Tajikistan and the Islamic Republic of Afghanistan dealing with economic and commercial cooperation to which the officials of branch ministries in charge were included.

To develop commercial and economic ties between the two states Tajik government adopted a number of resolutions on frontier trade where food stuffs and other consumer goods would be sold to the residents of IRA. Thus, on the initiative of the Ministry of Economy and Trade in 2002 the government adopted the edict "On Measures Aimed at Improvement of Tajik Frontier Area Trade" (No. 397 dated 2 October 2002) and decrees No. 400 dated 20 October 2002 and No. 436 of 8 October 2003 prescribing to make addendums and amendments in the edict mentioned above. The number of frontier trade units was increased as per the decrees specified.

In November 2002 in furtherance of the commission of Tajik government and on the authority of the Order of the Ministry of Economy and Trade a working team was formed to develop commercial and economic cooperation. According to the edict of the government they formed the State Commission for acceptance and maintenance of frontier trade units. In May 2005 frontier trade was officially launched in Darvaz, Khorog and Ishkashim. In July 2004 there was opened a trade mission of Tajikistan in Kabul. Since 2002 the whole number of agreements was signed between the two states. Unfortunately, many of them remained non-fulfilled.

The default of timely execution of resolutions is accounted for by objective and subjective reasons as well as by the unstable atmosphere in Afghanistan, unreciprocated attitude of ministerial officials of both states.

On the commission of Tajik government in 2003 the Ministry of Economics designed the drafts of agreements: "On Commercial and Economic Relations" and "On Propaganda and Inter-protection of Investments". The Afghan party submitted its own project "On Economy Cooperation" which was reviewed by the Ministry and respective departments followed by amendments and addendums and then delivered to the government of Tajikistan; the project was accepted in February 4, 2004 and signed in October 4, 2004 No. 45.

Following the stabilization of situation in Afghanistan goods turnover volume was tending towards growth as it is seen from the table below:

(in thousands USD)

	1999	2000	2001	2002	2003	2004	2005	2006-06-06
Export	2218,5	2579,1	3121,1	6341,7	6222,3	7677,5	12097,6	6644,3
Import	90,3	42,1	91,8	261,3	1594,3	3947,4	3358,9	2999,1
ITB	2308,8	2621,2	3212,9	6603,0	7816,6	11624,9	15,455	9643,4

Over the half year of 2005 this index averaged 6 925,4 thousand USD and for the six months of 2006—963,4 thousand US dollars.

It is worth mentioning that in export structure the prevailing items are transport vehicles, ferrous metal, its output, engineering industry products, technical and electric devices from the Republic of Tajikistan to the Islamic Republic of Afghanistan.

Data on external goods turnover between the Republic of Tajikistan and the Islamic State of Afghanistan in 2005:

(in thousands USD)

	2005
Total external turnover:	15501.4
Including:	
Export	12142,5
Import	3358,9
Difference	+ 8783,6

including export from the Republic of Tajikistan to the Islamic Republic of Afghanistan:

Code	Description of products	In thousands USD
3102	Mineral and nitrogen fertilizers	3 229
8703	Motor cars and other types of transport vehicles	2 004
2710	Petroleum and its derivatives	2 105
8704	Conveyance-loading motor vehicles	817
2716	Electric power	740

including export from the Islamic Republic of Afghanistan to Tajikistan:

Code	Description of products	In thousands USD
0805	Fresh and desiccated citrus plants	1 305
8703	Motor cars and other types of transport vehicles	499
8704	Conveyance-loading motor vehicles	490
2402	Cigarettes and tobacco	448

The list of signed bilateral intergovernmental documents: [17]

Description of documents	Place and time of signing	Notes
1. Agreement on friendship, cooperation and mutual aid between RT and IRA	Dushanbe 22.12.1993	Revision required
2. Agreement on frontier between RT and IRA	Dushanbe 22.12.1993	Revision required
3. Agreement on cooperation between RT and IRA in the spheres of culture, science and education	Dushanbe 22.12.1993	Revision required
4. Agreement between RT and IRA in the field of electric power	Dushanbe 21.01.2000	Effective
5. Agreement between "Focus" (humanitarian aid), RT and IRA governments on construction of bridge over the Pyandzh River.	Dushanbe 04.07.2001	Effective

6. Agreement between RT and IRA on air communications	Kabul 06.08.2002	Effective
7. Agreement between RT and IRA on opening Tajikistan Consulate in Mazar-i-Sharif and Afghan Consulate in Khorog	Dushanbe 26.11.2002	Effective
8. Agreement between RT and IRA governments on construction of bridge and its maintenance	Dushanbe 10.02.2004	Effective
9. Agreement between RT and IRA governments on commercial cooperation	Dushanbe 13.09.2004	Validated as per the edict of Tajik government dated 29 June 2005. No. 34

Documents	Date of signing
1. Treaty of Friendship, Cooperation and Good Neighborliness between RT and IRA governments	03.03.2005
2. Agreement between RT and IRA on bilateral provision of roperty for RT Embassy in Kabul and IRA Embassy in Dushanbe	28.10.2005
3. Agreement on mutual support and protection of investments	10.03.2005 unsigned
4. Agreement on non-admittance of double taxation	01.03.2005
5. Agreement on non-visa treatment with diplomatic passports	29.03.2005
6. Agreement on cooperation in the branch of electric power	29.03.2005
7. Agreement on cooperation in culture, science and education	29.03.2005
8. Agreement on cooperation in military sphere	29.03.2005
9. Agreement on shipment and unloading, transit of freights and passengers (Afghan version with Tajik amendments)	29.03.2005
10. Agreement on cooperation in industry	29.03.2005
11. Agreement on cooperation in the fight with illegal drug trafficking	29.03.2005
12. Agreement on cooperation in the fight with terrorism	01.04.2005
13. Agreement on frontier entry points	01.04.2005
14. Agreement on intentions concerned with bilateral coordinations (meetings) between Foreign Affairs Ministers of RT and IRA.	04.04.2005

Basic Streamlines of Commercial and Economic Cooperation between the Republic of Tajikistan and Islamic Republic of Afghanistan

In the sphere of commercial and economic cooperation:

- promoting of the Joint Commission activity on commercial and economic cooperation aimed at qualifying priority directions and designing actual difficulties;
- adjustment of frontier trade and enhancement of its efficacy;
- development of necessary measures for adjustment of productive cooperation;
- cooperation in the field of telecommunications services and communications;
- establishment of joint ventures in various spheres;
- organizing of exhibitions related to the products of enterprises and companies of RT and IRA;
- cooperation in the branch of economy information exchange;
- exchange of delegations representing the chambers of commerce;
- organizing of specialized seminars on development of economic cooperation between the two states;
- support of economic cooperation;

In the sphere of power engineering:

- organizing of meetings with responsible officers of IRA Ministry of Power Engineering and Water Resources bound to specify the construction and maintenance of Dashti Juma power station on the inter-frontier Pyandzh (Amu Darya) River aimed at power generation and irrigation of lands in both countries; power transmission lines (PTL) from Tajikistan to Afghanistan being implied as well;
- participation in implementation of the project on restoration of hydropower engineering constructions of Afghanistan funded by foreign states and organizations; here refer such objects as: Talukan-Faizabad PTL, Lolazor-Obi Mazor-Faizabad PTL, Kunduz-Baghlan-Puli-Khumri PTL; Karakuturma-Imom Sakhib PTL, Kunduz-Khonabad-Talukan PTL; reconstruction of Kunduz-Sadarak PTL and Darvaz-Shugnan PTL in Afghanistan;
- trilateral negotiations on reviewing the construction of 500 kW PTL Rogun-Kunduz-Puli, Khumti-Kabul-Jalalabad-Peshawar stretching from Afghanistan to Pakistan;
- exported sale of Tajik coal to the Islamic Republic of Afghanistan;

onsuring of practical delivery of gas from IRA to RT resolving the issue of stretching gas pipeline from Mazar-i-Sharif (Afghanistan) to Kolkhozabad (Tajikistan)—cooperation of "Tajikgas" state-owned enterprise with the Asian Development Bank (ADB) in this regard.

In the field of agriculture:

- organizing of trade exhibitions of the following products:
- soft drinks and mineral water;
- fruit juices, apples, grapes, apricots;
- tomatoes;
- confectionery (Iris, caramel) ;
- desiccated fruits;
- providing with highly quality seeds and fruit-tree seedlings (apples, grapes, lemons), development of apiculture; dissemination of cotton selection experience—these items being envisaged due to the similarity of climatic conditions and farming standards as mostly important ones.

In the sphere of banking and finances:
Proceeding from the importance of banking and finances it is important to establish cooperation in this sphere to ensure effective realization of the projects targeted to restoration of Afghanistan.

In industry:

- organizing of trade exhibitions of the products manufactured by Tajik enterprises in Afghanistan;
- utilization of Tajik industrial potential in production of goods for the Afghan market resorting to the resources of the state and donors in the frames of the agreements on post-conflict restoration of Afghanistan;
- development of cooperation in extraction and processing of ore, oil and gas, chemicals; light industry (weaving); manufacturing of furniture, ready-made clothes;
- development of cooperation with international organizations on procurement of the industrial products of Tajikistan for the population of Afghanistan in the framework of the humanitarian aid programs.

In the sphere of transport and goods transportation:

- establishment of new transport passage between three countries— Tajikistan, Afghanistan, Iran, including development of highway

- providing the route of Darogun-Shibirgan-Mazar-i-Sharif connected with the frontier of Tajikistan and repairs of its separate sections;
- joining Tajikistan and Afghanistan to the Agreement on utilization of the international transit road between Kazakhstan, Kyrgyzstan, People's Republic of China and the Islamic Republic of Pakistan signed in March 9,1995 in Islamabad;
- signing of the Agreement on the maintenance of waterways between the two countries;
- organizing of regular flights of "Tojikiston" Airline along the airways of Afghanistan.

In the sphere of public health service:

- development of diversified mutually beneficial cooperation with IRA in various streamlines of public health service, including training of medical personnel, sanitary epidemiology, mother and child protection, pharmaceutics, medical science and informational exchange;
- mutual exchange in experiences concerned with the study of new methods in diagnostics, prophylaxis and treatment of patients; cooperation in usage and research of the latest achievements in medicine, providing orthopedics to invalids;
- organizing of courses, seminars and trainings for professional development of medical staff;
- health service for the citizens of Afghanistan in medical institutions of Tajikistan, in the hospitals located on the frontier area; secondment of Tajik doctors to Afghanistan for rendering medical aid to its citizens, training of medical experts in educational institutions of Tajikistan.

In the sphere of education:

- designing and signing of draft agreements between the Ministry of Education of Tajikistan and the respective Ministry of Afghanistan on cooperation in the sphere of higher education, agreement between the Ministry of Education of Tajikistan and the Ministry of Education of Afghanistan on cooperation in the sphere of education, the protocol on cooperation between the Technical University of Tajikistan named after academician M. Asimov and Kabul Polytechnic University, protocol on cooperation between the State Medical University named after Avicenna and Kabul University (Puantun);

- granting availabilities for Afghan students in getting education at the Tajik National University, the Tajik State Medical University named after Avicenna, the Tajik Pedagogical University named after K. Juraev;
- meeting of the needs of the Afghan side in teachers out of Tajik specialists.

In the field of melioration and water industry:

- designing of the draft agreements between RT and IRA concerned with common water consumption in frontier areas;
- rendering engineering services in construction of the water supply objects, to supply the population, rural population especially, with drinking water by establishment of joint ventures;
- training of water industry specialists in the higher schools of Tajikistan and their involvement in the work of seminars and conferences held in RT;
- establishment of consulting services and development of projecting, exchange of experience in construction and maintenance of irrigative objects, supplying rural areas with drinking water;
- establishment of enterprises for manufacturing of glass-plastic pipes in Dushanbe utilizing our own resources to provide consumer market of IRA.

In combating drug trafficking:
To ensure coordinative actions it is necessary to open the representative offices of relevant authorities:

- development of cooperation fighting against illegal drug trafficking and their precursors.

In the sphere of cooperation between the interior agencies:

- opening of frontier service representative offices on the territory of both states;
- cooperation in fighting with illegal drug trafficking, development of joint actions plan to prevent of drugs export; designing of informational exchange mechanism in reference to the state of affairs concerned with illegal drug trafficking;
- coordination of the issues related to the problems raising between the frontier guards of Tajikistan and Afghanistan [19].

Notes:

1. Harakati Inqilobi Savr. 20 jadi, 366
2. RTSHIDNI, fund 89, index 42, doc.8—p.18
3. "Planeta za Nedelyu" (Weekly planet-revue), No. 103 dated November 12, 1987, p.12
4. The materials of the 27th Congress of CPSU-M:, Polytizdat,1986, p.327
5. "Planeta za Nedelyu" (Weekly planet-revue), No. 72 dated February 25, 1987, p.4
6. The Fund of multilateral ties department of current archives of Tajik Ministry of Interior.
7. National Economy of the Tajik SSR in 1990—Dushanbe, "Irfon", 1991.—p.13
8. ibidem,p.12
9. The reference of the State Committee of Tajik SSR "Figure Indices of Labor Resources Usage in the Tajik SSR". June 21,1988. The current archives of population employment center of the Republic of the Tajikistan
10. "Party Life" journal in Persian, 1988, No. 4,—p.84
11. Additional agreement on water borderline along the Amu Darya (Oxus) and Pyandzh Rivers. Central State Archives of the government of Tajikistan. Fund 1327, posted 3g. unit of storage 1.—p.111
12. Statistical collection "The State and Development of Economy and Culture of Democratic Republic of Afghanistan in 1984-1985". Kabul 1985.—p.9
13. RTSHIDNI, fund 89, index 14, doc.13-p. 4
14. "Planeta za Nedelyu" (Weekly planet-revue), No. 1-3 dated November 12, 1983
15. "Foreign Trade" journal 1987, M. No.10—p.22-23
16. The Fund of multilateral ties department of current archives of Tajik Ministry of Interior.
17. The tables given above, lists of documents, main streamlines of economic cooperation between RT and IRA are composed on the base of the materials referring to the current fund of International Ties Office of the Ministry of Economy and Trade of the Republic of Tajikistan for 2006.

PARAGRAPH 2

The Problems of Cooperation between Central Asian States in Post-Conflict Restoration of Afghanistan

Since the anti-terrorist operation commenced in Afghanistan, after the Taliban had gone away from the political arena the political objectives of Central Asian states in regard to this country started to undergo changes. At that these states proceed from both common regional interests being members of such alliances as Eurasian Economic Community, CIS, SCO and from those of UIK and ECA including Central Asian states together with Afghanistan. Yet in 2001 they created an alliance of Central Asian states for cooperation in the fight with terrorism having found the anti-terrorist Center to fight against terrorism.

The authorities of the region supported the states of the coalition in the fight with terrorism. Tajikistan, Uzbekistan and Kyrgyzstan have placed their territories as passages as well as the airdromes in Kulyab, Khanabad and Manas at the disposal of the USAF (later in Dushanbe-for France Air Forces) for conducting anti-terrorist operations.

The delegation of Tajikistan in UNO is a coauthor of the UNO program on disposal of power in ISA to the Interim Authority of Afghanistan.

For the last ten years the states of the region cooperated closely and consecutively to achieve national reconciliation in Tajikistan and Afghanistan. They have gained experience in peace-making. Their leaders called upon the United Nations Organization to promote to ensuring security and inviolability of frontiers between Afghanistan and Tajikistan and also to get involved in returning of refugees to their native homes [1].

Today, when a relative peace came to the severely suffering Afghan land all the leaders of Central Asian states are united in aspiration for peaceful co-existence and succeeding in regional security. They stand for making the region a nuclear-free zone. Kazakhstan signed and ratified the Treaty on non-proliferation of nuclear weapons and took a commitment to dismantle the strategic offensive nuclear weapon. All the leaders unanimously condemn terrorism and extremism, a sway of radical religious movement proceeding, as they deem, from contiguous Afghanistan.

The peoples of Tajikistan, Uzbekistan, Turkmenistan and Afghanistan since becoming the members of the Unified State of Khorasan preserved Islamic religion, linguistic similarity and common historic roots. Central Asian region and Kazakhstan enjoy enormous natural, energetic, water and labor resources, transport infrastructure and qualified specialists.

In the medium-term and especially long-term perspective some of the Central Asian states have good prerequisites at their disposal for ensuring of dynamic economic growth and integration into the world and regional economy as exporters of agricultural products and raw stuffs. To the point, already now Kazakhstan is a large-scale exporter of grain crops and a number of nonferrous metals; Uzbekistan is a cotton provider. Moreover, Uzbekistan is one of the world leading producers of gold. Rich resources of hydrocarbon raw stuffs impart global significance to the Central Asian economic complex. The matter mainly concerns Turkmenistan and Kazakhstan. Uzbekistan enjoying incomparably moderate resources of petroleum and gas, but being rich with gold, is close to these two countries in natural wealth.

The years 2004-2005 were mostly fruitful in this respect. In February 10, 2004 there was signed the agreement between the government of Tajikistan and the Interim Authority of Afghanistan "On Construction and Commissioning of the Bridge between RT and Afghanistan" (As for other intergovernmental agreements between RT and Afghanistan they are described in particulars in the previous paragraph).

The leadership of Uzbekistan strives for developing of mutual relations with Moslem states. Yet in September 2002 Islam Karimov sent an official invitation to the President of the Islamic State of Afghanistan B. Rabbani to visit Tashkent for holding intergovernmental negotiations.

The Uzbek-Afghan dialogue began fruitfully in Tashkent, since both parties revealed mutual understanding on many issues of bilateral and multilateral cooperation. The signing of the protocol on the establishment of diplomatic relations implied development of ties on the principles of mutual esteem and territorial integrity, non-interference into internal affairs, cooperation on the basis of equal rights and mutual benefits. There was achieved the agreement on improving of commercial, economic and cultural ties as well.

If the inner political situation in Afghanistan stabilizes there may appear "a geopolitical triangle" of which Afghanistan is bound to become a centre playing the role of a connecting link between Iran, Pakistan and Uzbekistan, including other independent states of Central Asia. In this respect we can add yet that through the Afghan territory Uzbekistan might enjoy the most economical route for delivery of its goods to the sea ports of Pakistan opening a further way to the regions of the Persian Gulf, Southern and South-Eastern Asia, etc.

At the meeting of I. Karimov with B. Rabbani they addressed also the issue concerned with lining of a broad highway which going through Afghanistan might link the Uzbek frontier town and river port of Termez with Pakistan ports Karachi and Kasim.

There was signed the agreement on air communications between Tashkent and Kabul as well.

In August 14-17, 1993 the official delegation of Afghanistan headed by the special envoy of President B. Rabbani, army General Abdul Rashid Dostum was in Tashkent. In the course of the conversation with the first deputy Prime Minister of Uzbekistan I. Jurabekov there were discussed the issues related with the further development and extension of commercial, cultural and scientific cooperation between the two countries. The members of the delegation held negotiations in the Ministry of external economic links, The Ministry of energy and electrification, the Ministry of melioration and water industry, in state concern "Uzavtodor" and other institutions [2].

Thus we can draw a conclusion that in perspective much broader multilateral cooperation between the Republic of Uzbekistan and the Islamic Republic of Afghanistan is quite possible. The both parties haven't yet exhausted their availabilities in mutual cooperation. Common state frontiers, history, culture, religion, language, customs and traditions invoke them for it.

Assistance in peace establishment in Afghanistan is the principal goal of the regional policy of Turkmenistan determined by its geopolitical and geo-economic interests. For Turkmenistan, just as for Tajikistan located in the closed geographic space, the territory of the southern neighbor is a transit passage enabling to move to the trade space of Southern and South-Eastern Asia. Yet in the Soviet times the Turkmen SSR and the Islamic Republic of Pakistan discussed the issue on lining a railway and automobile communications between Kushka (Turkmenistan), Gerat and Kandahar (Afghanistan) and Chaman (Pakistan).

Therefore, after the collapse of the USSR Turkmenistan has been seeking for alternative ways of entering into international markets of hydrocarbon raw-stuffs being the main source of its export. If now the capacity of two functioning pipelines exporting gas (Turkmenistan—Russia and Turkmenistan—Iran) does not exceed 60 billion cubic meters per annum natural gas resources in this country enable to provide an export of 100 billion cubic meters of raw stuff for one hundred years [3].

To meet the needs of Turkmenistan in the transportation of hydrocarbon raw stuffs to foreign markets multi-version pipeline infrastructure is needed. Its constituent part shoul be gas and petroleum pipelines bound to stretch from Turkmenistan through the territory of Afghanistan in the direction of Pakistan [4].

In addition, there was designed the feasibility study of PTL in 500 kW capacity bound to stretch along the route of Mary (Turkmenistan)—Shibirgan (Afghanistan)—Kabul-Peshavar [5]. Realization of these projects will promote to creation of favorable economic conditions both for Turkmenistan and Afghanistan.

By the end of the 1990s the volume of annual goods turnover between these two states amounted to 100 million dollars. Along the territory of Afghanistan there was also carried out the transit trade between Turkmenistan and Pakistan, transfer of Turkmen liquefied gas and lint cotton, in particular.

Turkmen leadership exercised persistent efforts to cause interest on the part of neighboring republics of Central Asia having large fuel-energy resources to get involved in the projects on trans-Afghan pipelines.

In July 2000 S. Niyazov made a visit to Astana. The Presidents of two states discussed the prospects of regulating the situation in Afghanistan and debated on the issues of cooperation between Turkmenistan, Kazakhstan and Afghanistan concerned with realization of trans-Afghan construction projects. By this the leaderships of Kazakhstan and Uzbekistan came to the conclusion that regularization of the situation in Afghanistan and establishment of normal intergovernmental relations with it were actually impossible without contacts with the Taliban movement which presented the real force on the military-political arena of Afghanistan [6].

In early March 2002 the head of Afghan government paid a visit to Turkmenistan. The leaders of the two states discussed a number of activities on restoration of the Afghan economy. The agreements achieved envisage mainly the continuation of commercial and economic cooperation within already shaped framework. The Turkmen side confirmed the agreement on proceeding with electric power deliveries to Afghanistan. In the course of negotiations they also discussed the perspectives of extending the frontier area trade and a transit of goods from Turkmenistan and other Central Asian countries along the territory of Afghanistan. The parties stood for the quickest revival of the projects concerned with construction of trans-Afghan pipelines.

In the nearest perspective commercial and economic ties of the two countries will cover such traditional spheres of cooperation as delivery of electric power, natural gas, oil products by Turkmenistan as well as frontier trade. As for the wide-scale usage of the Afghan territory as a transit passage to enter the markets of the southern Asian countries, and especially to export fuel-energy resources, settlement of this problem for Turkmenistan depends on normalization of the situation in Afghanistan.

Kyrgyzstan can carry into effect its commercial and economic ties with Afghanistan utilizing the transport infrastructure (passages) of Tajikistan.

In its foreign policy the Kyrgyz Republic coordinates the actions on combat with drug trafficking, international terrorism and religious extremism with the partners from CIS, Eurasian Economic Community and SCO.

In the political life of the Afghan society there occur important events. Hamid Karzai's Interim Authority created after a relative neutralization of Taliban began to do the first steps on stabilization and democratization of social life. In late March 2004 the representatives of 60 countries-donors assembled in Berlin to determine the availabilities of investing the projects on post-conflict restoration of Afghanistan. They develop and implement numerous projects on restoration of destroyed economy, habitation, educational and public health institutions, roads, communications and etc. The authorities of the country ask the world community to provide financial support counted in the tens of billions dollars for these needs.

In January 21-22 the International conference on the restoration of Afghanistan took place in Tokyo. It was attended by more than 60 countries and 20 international organizations. Counties-donors took commitments to render a considerable financial aid for the empty national treasury of Afghanistan. Leaving Kabul, Taliban took away all state-owned money in cash (over 200 million dollars).

The issue of importance is how the aid proposed will have been used. It is not an easy matter to spend this money properly. The past Soviet experience turned out to be ineffective: over 80% of the entire amount of food stuffs and medicines brought to Afghanistan from the USSR in late 1980s—early 1990s were wasted by officials both in Kabul and in Afghan provinces [7].

If the resources are distributed through Afghan authorities there may arise a great danger of their dissolving among numerous instances of various slants; abuses and purposeless application is quite possible. The mayor of Kabul Mohammed Anwar Jigdalak was dismissed from his post for these drawbacks. It would be reasonable to form something of a kind of an international committee in charge of aid for Afghanistan which would regulate entry of resources, pay foreign companies for specific works on construction or restoration of these or those objects. For example, many construction organizations of Central Asian states having no front of jobs, but being able to participate in international tenders would like to know the list of objects that need restoration provided the volume of jobs and equipment deliveries are indicated. It would help in determining the needs of the country and expend the allocated resources economically.

In due time the International Organization of Migration in Tajikistan in its work with refugees (over two million refugees having returned to Afghanistan for today) resorted to an addressed distribution of resources assigned for the restoration of destroyed dwelling houses. There is a grandiose work on restoration planned. But, unfortunately, the process of restoration of Afghanistan is hampered by a non-availability of a plan of its realization bound to be designed by the world community. For the time being only the USA determined the priority branches of their participation in this process: 1) agriculture; 2) power of law; 3) education; 4) health care; 5) program for women; 6) fight with drug trafficking.

As regards the Afghan government itself, Karzai's administration faced a great deal of problems—misery, political instability, drug trafficking, disarmament and mine clearing, return of refugees, formation of local authorities, restoration of the destroyed economy. Upon the whole, today the government focuses its endeavors on three streamlines: security, increase of initiatives and enthusiasm of the population (NGO's are being formed in the country). In Afghanistan where the war has been lasting over 25 years there accumulated a lot of arms and for many people fighting crystallized into a main occupation. Therefore, the measures of priority concern the realization of the program on arms withdrawal from population. But no wonder that this work has been going with difficulties. Even those wishing to yield arms don't know who and how will have utilized it. Strange as it may seem, arms are collected mainly in the northern part of the country. They motivate it by the statement that the arms kept by the population of the south-eastern part (Pashtuns being implied) will come in handy in the alleged fight with the remainders of Taliban and militant groups of Al-Qaida. The government tries to neutralize numerous commanders of divers ethnic groups; in their struggle for power the formers have been constantly provoking clashes. This struggle between field commanders and protégés of different political forces in the country subverts the structures of the central power and makes shadowed national contradictions transpire.

At the same time when implementing the programs of overcoming ethnic contradictions there evince insincerity and egoism of separate members of the government. Ostentatious provocations of confrontations between non-Pashtun national groups are used to fortify the positions of Pashtuns. It is common knowledge that non-Pashtun population prevails in Kabul. Here the so called "passport system" of population may cause a change in this correlation by means of integration of the Pashtuns who remove to the capital from provinces according to the organized plan; into the bargain, disguised Taliban entrenching themselves among common population can increase the number of "reliable voters". In their turn, the bordering Central Asian states should cease to display "solidarity" with their ethnic Diasporas. Here one ought to act in the framework of general regional politics aimed at stabilization of the situation in Afghanistan.

Meanwhile the struggle for power on the part of field commanders compels Karzai to maneuver maximally taking into account alignment of political forces in each region. He managed to work out a certain general principle of forming administration on sites. If the provincial population supports a certain local leader he is validated by the government, in case of conflict situation and rivalry between the leaders, Kabul refers another man as governor from the different province.

Notes

1. Miloslavsky G.V. Central Asia in Eurasian Perspective//Vostok/Oriens, 2002, No. 5. p.8
2. Kasimov, I. Vaskin. Basic Trends of Foreign Policy of the Republic of Uzbekistan. Tashkent. "Uzbekistan" 1994. p. 81-82
3. Neutral Turkmenistan newspaper, 29.03.2000. Ashgabat. 29.03.2000
4. Afghanistan in Transition Stage (September 2001-June 2002) M. CJSC "ASTI-IZDAT" printing-house. p. 172
5. Turkmenistan Today and Tomorrow.—Ashgabat. 1999. p. 47-48
6. Nezavisimaya Gazeta (Independent Newspaper). M. 27.09.2000
7. Afghanistan in Transition Stage (September 2001-June 2002) CJSC "ASTI-IZDAT" printing-house. M. 2002 p. 31

PARAGRAPH 3

Economic Needs and Demands of Afghanistan and Real Potentialities of Utilizing the Resources of Central Asian States in Its Post-War Restoration

The Afghan economy is in an extremely difficult plight, the drought of three years at a running resulted in mass mortality of cattle, especially in southern provinces, and crop failure; hereby the population was bound to be supported. In the past, before the war, being a traditional agrarian country, Afghanistan replenished the half of GDP with agriculture produce. But today up to 10 million various mines clot the fields of the country and they should be cleared first before cultivation. Here Kazakh experts holding their battalion of sappers in Iraq might come to succor, just as their Uzbek colleagues may.

Hundreds of kilometers lined with irrigating nets require restoration. In the past a great experience of cooperation between Central Asian republics in this branch was gained. In accordance with the agreement on the main streamlines of cooperation in the terms of direct ties for 1991-1992 signed between the Tajik SSR and Afghanistan, Tajik geologists and water consumption experts rendered assistance to Afghan organizations in construction of hydraulic objects and designing the schemes of land tenure in Northern Afghanistan. At that time the measures indicated enabled to increase the squares of watered pastures for 600 thousand hectares. Tajik experts together with their Soviet colleagues participated in the projects concerned with construction of 33 artesian wells and 115 shaft wells.

No less important goal is to restore the power potential of the country. And if for Northern provinces this problem may be settled fairly quickly at the expense of power delivery from Tajikistan (or from Turkmenistan for the eastern part) where it is relatively cheap—the cost of 1 kW/hour not exceeding USD 0,07 [1], the situation is complicated for the central region with one and a half

74

million population of Kabul and a number of industrial enterprises. If power engineering experts of Central Asian states get down to tackling technical issues the construction of the longest PTL in Afghanistan may solve all the problems with energy supply in reference to the Central region and the capital of the country. Hamid Karzai's comprehension of the importance is evidenced by the negotiations held by Tajik and Afghan colleagues. These problems were the subject of discussion during the official visit of the President of Tajikistan Emomali Rahmon to IRA in late April (early May) and the visit of IRA President Hamid Karzai to Tajikistan in late July 2006.

For the development and restoration of power engineering in Afghanistan Tajikistan together with Russia and Japan offered Afghanistan the project proceeding with the construction of Roghun power station in Tajikistan conserved in the 1990s because of poor finances, the capacity in 3600 thousand kW would enable to transport a part of power to Afghanistan along the available power lines. At that if only 5 % of capacity is conveyed to Afghanistan this country will get over a billion of kW/h, it exceeds all the electric power worked out in the pre-war years for 18.3% Tajikistan and Uzbekistan supply with electricity Kunduz and Mazar-i-Sharif.

The closeness of Tajikistan and Afghanistan enables to effect trading transactions on gas with the least losses. There shapes the situation when ISA restoring its industrial enterprises needs electric power and Tajikistan is in want of Afghan gas. Under the circumstances when the currency resources in both countries are limited (but for ISA gas remains one of the basic items of budget revenue) the option befalls exchange on the basis of mutually acceptable terms and conditions.

Geological explorations conducted on the territory of Afghanistan within the period from late 1950s up to the middle of the 1980s revealed the proximity of geological structures between the northern areas of Afghanistan and the southern regions of Central Asian states.

Realization of the project on gas and oil delivery from Turkmenistan to Pakistan may constitute an important article for the development of fuel base of the country, at that 850 km of the gas pipeline and 650 km of the oil pipeline will stretch along the territory of Afghanistan. According to calculations annual revenue from implementation of this project may average the sum of about 100-110 million dollars. A potentiality of the project being carried into effect in high enough, since out of 6.6 trillion cubic meters of natural gas deposits in Central Asia over 72 % befall Turkmenistan (2.9 trillion cubic meters) and Uzbekistan (91.9 trillion cubic meters), the countries being extremely interested in its export.

The Asian Development Bank allocated 1,5 million dollars for gas transit along the western part of Afghanistan from Turkmenistan to Pakistan.

From times immemorial one of important fuel products in Afghanistan was fire-wood. The importance of fuel products and fairly great demands for them in urban areas of the North is testified by the event when frontier trade between Afghanistan and Tajikistan was opened in 2000 in the vicinities of Badakhshan being held on certain days and Afghan entrepreneurs displayed prior interest in diesel fuel. Tajik vendors of fuel for the frontier market reacted immediately, they started to enhance the cost of the commodity first for 60%, and then for 100 %.

Upon completion of constructing of the bridges over the Pyandzh River from Tajikistan to Afghanistan it will be possible to connect with the most important trunk-roads stretching through Afghanistan from Central Asia and Iran in the direction of India with crossing Pakistan.

River basins separate Afghanistan from all neighboring countries: Amu Darya and the Pyandzh rivers. Central Asian states make a natural border with the states not only by the Amu Darya, but by the Syr-Darya either. Over-measured utilization of these two rivers poured into the swallowing of the Aral Sea. If Afghanistan used all the water it claims for, it might have led to confrontation with its Central Asian neighbors; the latter being already anxious for potential Afghan challenges in regard to water. Afghan representatives disapproved the actions of the Soviet authorities who strove after an augmentation of the cotton gross; in their opinion, the multitude of artificial water storages on the Central Asian side of the Amu Darya and the Pyandzh resulted in the erosion of the littoral Afghan soil.

Therefore, rational utilization of ebbing water resources requires joint regional cooperation.

Before the anti-terrorist operation in Afghanistan bordering states together with their allies tried to balance the presence of Pakistan by dint of supporting the Northern Alliance. Apart from the support proceeding from the bordering states separate armed groups functioning up to now rely on foreign ethnic ties, parallel economy and drug trafficking. The new routes through Central Asia are opened in addition to the existing trading ways through Pakistan and Iran to the Persian Gulf or Turkey. In the outcome the number of registered drug addicts in Central Asia according to the data of the United Nations accreted from 16 % in 1992 to 28 % in 2000. As a result in five Central Asian states they mustered approximately 400 000 people using opium and heroin. To achieve any effective results in the combat against drug trafficking, it is important to establish cooperation in the framework of both functioning structures and new supranational regional ones as well.

For the time being the influential figures in the government of Afghanistan and a part of Afghans accuse the interference of the bordering countries of Central Asia alongside with Pakistan and Iran in their problems being cautious in relations with the neighbors. In 2002 the government of Afghanistan focused its attention on cooperation with the United States and UNO—main donors-investors. The government project "National Development Frames" did not include regional cooperation. Trading strategy was targeted basically at the markets of the developed countries. Meanwhile Afghans have been discussing how centralized their future government should be, a great number of common citizens propose a sample of restoration project bound to strengthen local governance based on associations with the neighboring countries. For the time being Central Asian states wishing to have profits from restoration still apprehend of opening their frontiers in the South as it may eventuate into drug trafficking extension and illegal arms trade they wouldn't be able to control.

Regional cooperation is more probable in some other fields. Cooperation on the issues of security, apart from specific anti-terrorist actions, seems to be the mostly actual sphere of cooperation. Most likely due to the history of mutual relations with Afghanistan the bordering states were admitted for participation neither in the International Security Forces nor in the actions of the USA and Europe on the formation of Afghan national security forces. Broad international guarantees for security will be in need for a regional cooperation in other spheres as well. Some countries stood even for the formal neutrality in reference to Afghanistan, Austria for instance. "If all neighbors consent to respect Afghan neutrality nobody should meddle in avoidance of rivalry"—Austrians believe.

For the latest 20 years many Afghans graduated higher schools of Central Asian states having been awarded diplomas of doctors, teachers, agronomists, engineers etc. They reside both in Afghanistan and in the neighboring republics having remained there as refugees. Now as never before there is a great demand for them to restore economy, to reanimate education, to regenerate spiritual life of their country.

For the years of independence different international organizations carried out all types of projects in the Central Asian countries: poverty reduction, support of entrepreneurship, civil education, development of economy, reforms of education and public health etc. There are regional projects too. Thus, in 1997 the Asian Development Bank started to develop the project in Central Asia on exploration of the technical state of the transport, trade, power and water resources. A soon enforcement of Central Asian Economy Cooperation Program is bound to be commissioned into operation including the states of Central Asia as well as Azerbaijan and China. In the course of realization of numerous projects designed by international organizations and banks (those of the World Bank, European Bank, Asian Development Bank and Islamic Bank) the experience of chiefs and experts dealing with these projects might be used in the process of post-conflict restoration of Afghanistan.

For regional cooperation with Afghanistan there are certain impediments: differences in customs rules, disproportion of trade regulations, non-identity of state structures and legislative foundations. The states of the region to a greater extent are turned to cooperation with rather developed countries than to cooperation with neighboring states. Therefore, the initiatives of the mentioned states for coordinating their actions in establishment of regional foundations and relevant structures for restoration of Afghanistan are considered more moderate. It comes as no surprise that many international forums devoted to Afghanistan are held in Bonn, Tokyo, Berlin, but not in the cities of any neighboring region.

The leaders of Central Asian states associate the stability in their own republics with the political atmosphere in Afghanistan. Therefore, regional cooperation ought to be the matter of priority for reinstatement of stability in this country and stability in Afghanistan ought to be the priority for regional cooperation.

Notwithstanding separate contradictions which generated mutual suspicions and mistrust, nevertheless, we shall have to live as good neighbors on the principles of territorial integrity, mutual respect and non-interference into internal affairs. There is nothing else to be done.

Notes:

1. T.N. Nazarov. Tajikistan: Economic Cooperation and Security. Minsk, 2003. RUP "Belpolygraph", p.155
2. "Asia-Plus" paper. July, 2006
3. Barnet Rubin and Andrea Armstrong. Regional Issues in the Reconstruction of Afghanistan. 37

CHAPTER 4

On the Issues of Spiritual and Cultural Cooperation between the Republic of Tajikistan and the Islamic Republic of Afghanistan

Relative peace has been coming to the Afghan earth. Tajikistan also experienced civil war and it is gradually recovering its wounds having pursued the way of the reconstruction of its economy which sustained chaos and crisis after the collapse of the USSR followed by the fratricidal war.

Today when a relatively quiet political situation established on the long-suffering Afghan earth definite conditions take shape for the reinstatements of friendly ties, laying of grounds for infrastructure, lining of transnational roads bound to connect Tajik cities with Gerat and with other Afghan cities through Gerat. They are constructing several bridges over the Pyandzh which will connect Tajikistan with Afghanistan. Now regular air flights connect Dushanbe and Kabul.

Regular contacts between the heads of the neighboring states take place in the sphere of politics; they participate in the work of regional organizations of ECO, OIC and Eurasian Economic Community.

The President of Tajikistan Emomali Rahmon declared 2006 to be the Year of Aryans.

The meetings and symposiums of Persian language and literature teachers from Tajikistan, Afghanistan and Iran aimed at improvement of their studies turned into tradition.

Comparing the achievements of our republic for the years of the Soviet power Afghans were always enraptured with the bloom of our culture, urban building, education and science. I myself heard repeatedly from Afghans that for them Tajikistan is like Mecca.

The desire of independent Tajikistan to have amicably inclined neighbors, including Afghanistan, is quite natural, and as for our southern neighbor, we are associated with it by the community of cultures, history and religion.

In the 4th-5th centuries the northern and eastern parts of Iran were renamed into Khorasan. This administrative formation included the north-eastern part of contemporary Iran, the greater part of northern Afghanistan and considerable part of Central Asian territory.

Later on, Samanid dynasty formed on this area in the 9th-10th centuries achieved an impetuous efflorescence of economy, science and culture. It is this historic period when cultural renaissance of the Tajik-Iranian peoples residing in the eastern part of the then state of Iran occurred.

The historical facts in the form of manuscripts, books, landmarks testify to the fact that this region granted the world civilization with the enormous pleiad of the science, art and culture coryphaeus. They wrote their masterpieces in Dari, but belonged to Tajiks.

The historic process resulted in the outcome into the situation that the unified ethnic community which existed in the old days up to the state of the Manghit dynasty (1753-1920) was discontinued. The Great trading road crossed these two states and connected them in the course of centuries. There are common traditions, common experience of good neighborly relations between the peoples inhabiting now Tajikistan and Uzbekistan which can be traced back into the depth of centuries.

Khwarezm, Zerafshan, Sughd, Gerat, Merv, Bukhara, Khujand, Helmand, Kabul refer to the Aryan civilization. Many historic monuments of culture found in these cities, literary works of classics belonged to the peoples of the both countries.

Tajik and Afghans residing on the both banks of the Amu Darya had common culture, architecture, calligraphy, science, literature, music. Linguistic community promoted much to it. Since the 7th century in spite of aggression and the Arabic conquest of the present territories of Tajikistan and Afghanistan, the language being common for the peoples who inhabited these areas, the Dari language was not assimilated having withstood.

Historic facts testify to the fortunes of Afghans and Tajiks being interwoven.

Hoshim Shoik, Tajik, an Ambassador of Bukhara People's Republic in Kabul, after the transformation of the mentioned Republic in 1924 remained in Afghanistan, he occupied the post of a chief of the Office under the Ministry of Education of Afghanistan.

When under the influence of the Great October revolution liberation movement deployed in Pashtunistan, the teacher Nisor Mohammad became an organizer of the national-patriotic movement for the liberation of Pashtunistan, he displayed unprecedented heroism equal to exploit in the war against the

English invaders. Later on he was elected a member of the Indian revolutionary organization. After the disintegration of the given organization in 1920 Nisor Mohammad entered the International propagandistic Council in the Tajik-speaking regions of Middle Asia and came forward in support and defense of the Soviet state. He opened Tajik schools in Samarqand, Khujand, Kanibadam and Fergana. Being the author of the first "Primer of the Tajik Language", evincing laboring valor in the period of 1924-1932 he was referred to Moscow for studying at the Institute of Oriental studies under the Academy of Sciences of the USSR as a post-graduate; on returning he worked as a Minister of Education of the Tajik SSR.

The relations with Afghans were different in the course of times, being complicated, contradictory, non-wrapped in a single concept.

In 1924 in the welcome message addressed to the Afghan leaders through its Embassy in Kabul the government of the Tajik autonomous republic included at that time into the Bukhara Soviet Republic noted: "the independent Republic of Tajikistan being an integral part of the USSR will in every possible way promote the solidity and development of economic and cultural cooperation between Tajikistan and Afghanistan [1].

Our cultural ties enjoyed the utmost upsurge in the sixties of the century passed and were continued up to the period of the communistic government in Afghanistan when NDPA was in power. Our ties bore a multilateral character embracing such spheres as literature, art, science, television, cinema, press, book publication, museum, sports.

The ideological interests of the country, including the Tajik SSR, made Soviet politicians tackle the issues of cooperation in regard to book publication, as well as Arabic print being in need, so as to bring works of the men-of-letters of Tajikistan not only to the notice of contemporaries, but of the population of Iran and Afghanistan either. When NDPA governed in the country the developed polygraph publishing base of Tajikistan enabled to arrange and issue 11 types of manuals for Afghan schools and a lot of belles-lettres books in Dari language. Since 1960 and up to 1973 5 thousand copies of books, works of the writers and poets of Tajikistan, 800 copies of manuals for studying Russian language, 1300 copies of the Russian primer were sent to Afghanistan. "Irfon" publishing-house issued the outstanding works of Soviet scientists dwelling on social and economic, literary and art, moral themes for Afghan readers in Dari.

The important event in the cultural life of the peoples of both countries was inception of creating the multi-volume history of the Asian people' civilization in 1997 in pursuance with UNESCO resolution.

When the producers invited to the theatre of Kabul from the USA and West Germany hadn't satisfied the aesthetic needs of the Afghan public, and the Ministry of Culture invited a producer from Tajikistan. The theatrical circles of Kabul are still grateful to the Tajik producer Mehrubon Nazarov for his long-term assistance in mastering the system of Stanislavsky by the Kabul Nandari theatre. In the course of long business trip to Afghanistan he performed over 23 plays of Afghan, Tajik, Russian classics and other European playwrights.

The great events in the cultural life of Tajikistan were the tours of the Kabul theatre "Pukhani Nandari" in Dushanbe in 1965; alongside with the plays of Afghan dramatists the repertory included "Shinel" ("The Greatcoat") by N.V.Gogol, "Medved" ("The Bear") by A. Chekhov, "Bez Viny Vinovatiye" ("Guilty without Guilt") by A. Ostrovsky.

In Tajikistan the songs of the famous Afghan singers gained popularity, among them there are Ogoya Khayol, Ahmad Zahir, Sarban, Sarmast, Khanoma, Mahwash and others.

The soloists of "Zebo" choreographic ensemble, singers Surayo Kosimova, Nigina Raupova, Manizha, Odina Khoshim, Zafar Nozim and many others won the affection of Afghan people.

We remember that the tours of our actors in Afghanistan went on in rather tense, restless situation. But in Kabul where hundreds of terrorist acts, murders and plunders occurred daily there was no incident and provocation. Indeed, beauty will have saved the world.

Joint celebration in honor of jubilee dates of outstanding coryphaei and stars of science and poetry of Asia became a good tradition: A. Rudaki (1100 years), Hafez Shirazi (650 years), A. Jami (550 years), Avicenna (1000 years), S. Aini (100 years), the remarkable classics of the Pashtun literature Khushholkon Hattaki and poet Khalilullo Khalili, Tajik poet Mirzo Tursunzade and many others.

The Afghan journal "Zhvandun" in the article published in 1981 called Mirzo Tursunzade's poem "Golos Azii" ("The Voice of Asia") a hymn to the awakening of the peoples of the Orient.

When in 1958 they celebrated the 40th anniversary of the independence of Afghanistan having invited an imposing delegation of the masters of arts of Tajikistan in the period of the tours an unprecedented event occurred. At the concert of the popular hafiz Aka Sharif Juraev organized on the request of Afghan women his signing produced such an emotional impression that the latter jerked down the curtain covering females from a male actor according to local customs.

Some people compared the sojourn of Russian frontier guards in the past with something of this sort as if it hampered the intercourse between two neighboring peoples. Probably, it reflects the viewpoint of definite circles, such as Basmachi who migrated here from Tajikistan in 1930s, contemporary drug criminals, those nationalistic, separatist and extremist religious groups like Hizb-ut-Tahrir dreaming of creation of some unified state of Khorasan. To what extent are their intentions realistic?

The Islamic revolution in Iran (1978-1979), the downfall of the communist's regime and the advent of mujahideen to power couldn't have helped to exercise influence upon the minds of the religious clergy and a certain part of the intellectuals in Tajikistan. This was promoted by ideological disarmament of population associated with the collapse of the USSR and the formation of something like weltanschauung vacuum.

The suspension of the CPSU activity and the collapse of the dominating ideology with bellicose atheism eventuated in a revival of the spirit of fundamentalism and the ideas of the export of revolution from contiguous countries.

With the establishment of the theocratic power after the revolution in Iran in 1978 its leadership didn't conceal its intention to export the Islamic forms of governance to other countries of the world. Imam Homayni invoked in his bequest: "Move to Islamic state organizing independent republics, since with their establishment you will curb all world aggressors and bring all the indigent to Islamic governance" [3].

Ex-Minister of Foreign Affairs of Iran Ali Akbar Viloyati in his article "The New View to the History of Middle Asia" wrote: "Having the rich ancient history after the collapse of the USSR we must exercise all our efforts to help Central Asia and the Caucasus to return into a natural world cultural civilized channel their forefathers enjoyed in the past".

Spiritual and religious solidarity between the populations of the neighboring countries have more vividly evinced in the years of the civil war in Tajikistan.

Due to the timely active political drives on the part of Russia and other CIS countries it became possible to preserve spiritual values of the people—culture, education, way of life—achieved for the years of the Soviet power from the destructive, radical religious influence proceeding from the contiguous states. But today Tajikistan participation in Eurasian Economic Community and SCO is bound to decrease a probability of radical forces coming to power in Tajikistan and of refusal from the principles of secular state.

Not only Islamic forces in Tajikistan itself, but the Tajiks of Afghanistan either are concerned with the relations between Tajikistan and Afghanistan to get warmer. In the complicated political struggle continuing to sever Afghanistan into isolated areas ethnic Tajiks have to seek for partners in Central Asian region and in Tajikistan, in particular.

The analysis of the situation in Tajikistan doesn't give convincing methods of sway over confessional sphere on the part of Afghanistan where the majority of political movements and parties in force, including radical ones, are Islamic.

What is the role of Islamic factor in Tajik-Afghan relations? As the whole, the status of the population in regard to religion is different in the two countries. Durable ascendancy of different social and political formations, framework, contradicting ideologies accounts for it. The creation of the Islamic State of Afghanistan is preconditioned with the whole course of its historic development in the patriarchal, semi-feudal social framework accompanied with a corresponding way of life and a respective outlook. In Tajikistan after gaining independence, they created a secular state where all citizens are entitled freedom of persuasion. In our state with multiple religious beliefs citizens profess different persuasions: Islam, Orthodoxy, Judaism, Bahai and others.

Here the civilized-cultural rupture between the peoples of Afghanistan and Tajikistan, identical in religion and kindred in ethnic respect, might have played a significant role.

For the years of the Soviet power in Tajikistan there were raised several generations of people with secular materialistic consciousness, respective morality, modus vivendi being utterly incomparable with the outlook of Afghans.

In Central Asia in the period of communistic ideology domination there shaped a peculiar situation when the local community mingled with the European component. The Soviet modus vivendi, moral values and convictions imbued with the population of Tajikistan were guarded by the "iron curtain" of communistic ideology, more and more Tajiks estranged from the dogmatic Islamic belief inherent in the neighboring population of Afghanistan.

The erosion of communistic ideology started concurrently with the process of perestroika actualized the ethno-cultural and religious identities of Central Asia to search the bearings of the national idea; Islam being no exclusion.

In the entrails of the Afghan society with the outlook of its own the attitude to secular Tajikistan is not wrapped in a single concept.

It is accounted for by certain considerations. Under the communistic regime in Afghanistan the Soviet government used Tajiks mostly as advisors consulting NDPA, Ministry of Education, Ministry of Culture, and as interpreters of military service; retaining the distance which impeded from the contacts with the Tajik-speaking part of the Afghan population the Soviets pursued the policy of Tajikistan isolation from an ideological and religious influence of the contiguous neighbor.

Up to now Afghans have been harboring offence at Tajik military officers for their participation in military operations in Afghanistan when included into the contingent of the Soviet troops.

The correspondent of German newspaper on his visit to Dushanbe expressed surprise in his article with the position of Tajik intellectuals considering themselves as having common cultural roots for their utterly indifferent attitude to the intrusion of the Soviet troops into this country; at least, no smallest reaction being noticed on the part of Mass Media [4].

Today we seem to be likened in this respect to the similar situation, as the factor of hampering our ties is the presence of the anti-terrorist coalition and NATO on the territory of the state being our neighbor. Thus, in the North of Afghanistan the armed forces of Germany are deployed in the provinces contiguous with Tajikistan; in the West there is the military contingent of Italy and Spain; in the south there are Great Britain and Canada; in the East—the USA, 21 thousand people from forcing counties all in all [5].

The victims of the durable war which lasted twenty three years and relatives of three millions of the perished, many invalids and orphans, those who turned to be forced refugees—all of them are pervaded with feelings of revenge, fanaticism and hatred towards those who brought chaos, famine, sufferings into the habitual way of life, who took ideals and moral values away. In particular, it found its expression in the participation of Afghan militants in military operations against the lawful government in the period of the civil war in the South of Tajikistan.

It is hardly serious to rely on a kind of integration of these states taking into consideration different standards and features of development, mentality, outlooks etc.

It is common knowledge that in Afghanistan the population consisting of diverse ethnic groups, nevertheless, identifies itself only with Afghans and is imbued with respective national consciousness common for all at a running.

As is known the process of Pashtunization has been going on in Afghanistan. They wanted to translate the National Anthem into Pashto; Persian being infrequently subjected to discrimination. They say it is no problem if you write you are Tajik, it is no problem if you are resettled from Panjshir and other northern provinces and Pashtuns from the south will move to the north. They change the Tajik names of educational institutions.

The North in reference to culture and education had always been more developed as compared with the South and it would wrong to adopt laws and rules reducing northerners to the level of southerners. And the role of separate persons in these matters is of no small importance. Thus, Mr. Mohammad Khalilzay, a Pashtun from the clan of Mohammad Gul Momand known as the conqueror of Northern Afghanistan who annihilated Tajik intellectuals in Balkh was appointed as an Ambassador in the USA. He is famous as an instigator of interethnic conflicts in the contemporary Afghan society. If the United States do not withdraw their troops from the country the atmosphere may aggravate; if democratic methods and national justice are not ensured the situation will be shaping in favor of religious extremists of Al-Qaida.

Tajikistan as a young state is bound to design its own model of the future spiritual development with the Islamic factor being taken into account; to provide balance between secularity of the state and religious inclinations of the native population; one can't disregard the factor of being surrounded by Islamic states either. Bearing this peculiarity in mind one can hold in view an establishment of good neighborly relations between the peoples of Tajikistan and Afghanistan in the offing. And today muses keep silence because cannons thunder. In the South and the East of Afghanistan military collisions between the antigovernment forces and those of the coalition have been breaking out.

Notes:

1. Nazarov Kh., Rakhmatov I. Nazare ba ravobiti farhangii Tojikistonu Afghoniston (A Review of Cultural Ties between Tajikistan and Afghanistan). Donish, 1987.—p. 9
2. Nazarov Kh., Rakhmatov I. Nazare ba ravobiti farhangii Tojikistonu Afghoniston (A Review of Cultural Ties between Tajikistan and Afghanistan). Donish, Dushanbe. 1987.—p. 21
3. The Great Ayatolla Imam Homayni. "Bequest"/The edition is prepared by the independent informational center "Tavhid".—p.21. The bequest is signed by the author, Ruholla Musavi Homayni. Bakhman 26, 1341
4. General Anzeiger. March 19, 1994
5. BBC Broadcast dated August 19, 2006.

CHAPTER 5

Tajik-Afghan Frontier in the Context of Strengthening Regional Security in Central Asia

In autumn 2006 the Republic of Tajikistan celebrated the fifteenth anniversary of having gained independence. The people of Tajikistan had to survive hard times for the years passed. Joy and exultation of the early period were replaced soon with disappointment and obscurity. Against the background of the unleashed civil war the youngest newly-born country had to assume multitude of functions which in the Soviet times were implemented by the Union framework. Here refer: self-sufficient governance of the state, ensuring of defense and security, foreign policy pursuit, guard of frontiers and etc.

The young state confronted the necessity of reconstruction of the earlier established orders, of the system of self-sufficient governance in regard to all spheres of domestic and foreign policy and practice in the frames of the independence "granted" to us after the notorious agreements in Belovezhskaya Pushcha.

At that moment the author of these lines happened to be on business trip in Kabul and everywhere Afghans congratulated him on having acquired independence, but, evidently, due to the strength of the stable Soviet mentality the author perceived it not very sensitively. Surely, in spite of our ideological prejudices it was enough to fly by plane to Khorog passing the gorge over the Pyandzh River that divides the two states—Tajikistan and Afghanistan, when you saw a striking contrast which reflected progress and backwardness, archaic tenor and modern way of life.

But soon the flame of the civil war mushroomed over Tajikistan. At that time the sojourn of Russian frontier guard troops and the former 201 motor-shooting division was motivated by the inter-Tajik conflict and the tense situation on the

Tajik-Afghan border, as well as by the Treaty between the Republic of Tajikistan and the Russian Federation "On 201 Motor-shooting Division" and on "Legal Status of Frontier Guards of Russian Federation on the territory of the Republic of Tajikistan" dated May 25, 1993.

Today owing to the endeavors of the world community—UNO, Russia and Central Asian states it became possible not only to achieve peace and concordance in Tajikistan, but to strengthen national community and get down to peaceful creation either.

From the viewpoint of the international law, of course, the Republic of Tajikistan caused a precedent having permitted to guard its frontiers to the troops of another state.

In Dushanbe at the negotiations of the working team on the preparation for the visit of ISA President Burhanuddin Rabbani to the Republic of Tajikistan in 1993 I witnessed how the members of the Afghan delegation when scrutinizing the project of the documents moved an objection against the formulation which called our republic as an independent one, they motivated their remonstrance by the alleged guard of Tajikistan frontier by the troops of the foreign state. They could not comprehend the essence of the national interests of Russia in Middle Asia and why Russian troops in Tajikistan were to guard its frontier with Afghanistan; in their opinion, the former was set artificially in late nineteenth century having divided the possessions of Russian and British empires. The both ones ceased their existence; that being their principal argument.

The withdrawal of Russian frontier guards from Tajikistan was backed with OSCE, NATO, southern neighbors and remote foreign states.

It is natural the young state along with other arisen problems faced with that one of guarding its frontier self-sufficiently. It goes without saying that the withdrawal of Russian frontier guard troops from Tajikistan may elevate its international status, afford the republic to regulate self-sufficiently its foreign policy, to attract foreign investments, to extend cooperation with new partners. It is an objective process. But the task is no easy one. Tajikistan has contiguous frontiers with Uzbekistan, Kyrgyzstan, China and Islamic Republic of Afghanistan of the general stretch in four thousand km. The protection of the frontier with Afghanistan stretching for 1300 km causes especial anxiety. The goals and functions beset with frontier protection changed from time to time depending on vacillations in political situations both in Afghanistan and in Tajikistan.

The scrutiny of archive materials shows that up to 1987 at joint sessions of frontier commissioners of the USSR and Afghanistan such issues were considered mostly as: ponds for watering Afghan horses on the territories belonging to the Soviet side, gold-mining works, firewood procurement, incidents with postage delivery and other matters. Later on the motives and the character of transgressions began to change. Evidently, the consequences of long-run war, devastation and impoverishment made Afghans to commit such actions on the borderline as picking up of liquorices, they appeared on the islets of Tajikistan with the purpose of panning out some gold dust.

After the downfall of Najibullah's regime and the victory of mujahideen the military-political situation had changed and the border between Afghanistan and Tajikistan considered as friendly before conversed into a hotbed of armed provocations and constant tension. Yet since 1985 Afghan rebels perpetrated sallies in the direction of military posts and arsenals stationed on contiguous territories. Gradually frontier transgressions bearing an economic character commenced to be acquiring a patently political essence. In the days of mass meetings and tumults in Dushanbe in October 1991 in a number of borderline points in the North of the Republic of Afghanistan there were seen Afghan armed bands trying to approach the Tajik frontier, they declared about their promptitude to come to their Tajik brothers' succor in the defense of independence. The leader of the Democratic Party of Tajikistan of that time Sh. Yusupov in general stood for opening of the Tajik-Afghan border for unimpeded intercourse and cooperation in multilateral scope.

In 1991 there commenced direct subversions and murders of civilians in Ishkashim district of Gorno-Badakhshan Autonomous Region bordering on Afghanistan, interceptions of economy freights, capture of hostages out of military men for their subsequent exchange for food stuffs and arms.

The American weekly "News-week" reported in 1991 with reference to diplomatic and governmental sources that for the latest time there appeared Islamic semi-military formations in Tajikistan; the leader of Afghan mujahideen G. Hekmatyar being in charge of their training and armament. "News-week" wrote further that the sources believed in his having referred the arms to the republic ere long the USSR collapse surreptitiously.

The events followed confirmed this version. There is authentic information of the participation of Afghan mujahideen in Shahidon meetings in Dushanbe and their assistance in arms delivery. Having joined the Tajik armed opposition they fought against their coreligionists in Ramit, Karatog, Gorno-Badakhshan, Jilikul and Tavildara.

Extremist sallies were not infrequently accompanied by separatist declarations. Thus, the leader of the Islamic Alliance of Northern Provinces of Afghanistan (IANPA) Azad Bek stated, in particular: "Our motherland is Bukhara and our final purpose is establishment of a unified Islamic state involving the Moslems of Central Asian republics of the former USSR to our side". The same thing was being reiterated by Taliban leaders when seven years ago they seized the major part of Afghanistan and approached Tajik frontier from Farkhor and Moskovsky districts, they started to threaten with incursion into the bordering areas and carnage of its population.

For the latest time our separate compatriots who migrated to Afghanistan in the 1930s of 20th century are speaking with nostalgia about the lands of ancestors, laying emphasis on the locution: "evidently the trees planted by our grandfathers bring fruits, so, it's high time the harvest were picked up by us".

In their appeal to Afghan compatriots mujahideen broadcasted from America: " . . . oh, if only there existed a national government today which would move claims to the existing Soviet government proceeding from mujahideen to return us the lands in the North of Afghanistan, such as Pendin oasis and the areas around the Murghab River" [1].

Already in 1992 the Afghan opposition started to lay rigid demands for a full utilization of the Afghan quota in regard to the Amu Darya waters; but taking into account the scope of Afghan lands bound to be irrigated the challenge could not be satisfied, otherwise Central Asian republics would have been doomed to hunger rations.

But the matter was not limited only with separatist declarations. In the period of the civil war frontier guards had to repulse multiple endeavors of Afghan armed band formations to break through the frontier to the territory of sovereign Tajikistan.

In April 30, 2004 the President of Tajikistan Emomali Rahmon in his speech to Majlisi Oli (the Parliament) pointed to the enormous role that Russian frontier guards had played in the protection of the Tajik frontier. Only for the years of independence they lost about 200 soldiers and officers in battle clashes. The night from the 12th to the 13th of July 1993 entered history with a tragic line. The militants of the implacable Tajik opposition and Afghan mujahideen committed a provocative sally in the direction of the territory of sovereign Tajikistan and took away the young lives of 25 Russian fellows who served at outpost 12 subordinated to Moscow frontier guard detachment. At that period the frontier guards had to repel militants' assaults both from the front and rear.

In autumn 1995 the leadership of the Islamic Revival Movement of Tajikistan (IRMT) entered into agreement with the Taliban Islamic movement according to which after the seizure of Kabul and usurpation of power along entire Afghanistan Taliban were bound to help IRMT in assuming power in Republic of Tajikistan and to establish an Islamic regime there. However, later Taliban dissolved the agreement. Rabbani's government didn't forgive IRMT such a betrayal. "The Afghan problem is Russian problem too. Those who stand behind the backs of Taliban are interested not only and not to such extent in Afghanistan . . ."—the leader of the Islamic Movement of Afghanistan, General Abdul Rashid Dostum stressed in his interview to press in May 19, 1997. Russia is also confident in the danger for its national security.

Only for 2003 Russian frontier guard detachments were subjected to firing 12 times, both from the territory of contiguous Afghanistan and from that of Tajikistan; they went into battle clashes 25 times and not infrequently frontier transgressors dominated in force. For the period of 2003 and 8 months of 2004 over 200 citizens of Afghanistan were detained for having violated the frontier;

hundred of them being imprisoned in Tajikiotan. They are sentenced for arms smuggle and drugs.

What is the state of affairs for today? What can be anticipated at the frontier tomorrow? During his official visit to Tajikistan in October 16-17, 2004 the President of Russia Vladimir Putin and the President of Tajikistan E. Rahmonov along with the set of documents signed the Agreement on cooperation in regard to frontier guards. In December 5, 2004 Russian frontier guards terminated the withdrawal of their subdivisions from the Pamirs. In 2005 Moscovsko-Shurabadsky (200 km), Pyandzh and Shaartuz (400 km) outposts were transmitted under the jurisdiction of Tajik "green caps".

Russian frontier guards not only protected the frontiers of Tajikistan, but they ensured the security of CIS outer borders. Therefore, in connection with stage-by-stage withdrawal of Russian frontier guards from Tajikistan the latter were in anxiety wishing to know: Why? What and how is it going to happen? What consequences can be envisaged? What is the attitude of the main "players" towards this important political event? . . . and a lot of other things being remained unknown.

The President of the Republic of Tajikistan Emomali Rahmon pointedly raised the issue of jointly coordinated actions on the part of international and regional organizations in the struggle against extremism in general and that one proceeding from Afghanistan, in particular; he used all the tribunes he had at his disposal, beginning with UNO sessions, CIS, SCO and Eurasian Economic Community summits and many others.

Ere long mass subversive terrorist actions in Tashkent and other cities and towns of Uzbekistan perpetrated by Islamic Jihad of Uzbekistan, Hizb-ut-Tahrir and other band formations which entrenched themselves in Afghanistan, yet in June 1992 the President of Uzbekistan Islam Karimov initiated a suggestion at CIS summit in Tashkent on fortifying the Tajik-Afghan frontier plot with additional forces [2].

Later at Istanbul conference of the Economy Cooperation Organization in 2003 when the heads of Tajikistan and Afghanistan met together there was reached an agreement on forming a four-sided commission including such countries as Afghanistan, Tajikistan, Uzbekistan and Russian Federation to address the frontiers related issues.

Intensive war clashes on the Tajik-Afghan border continued up to 1994 until the agreement on temporal cessation of firing and other hostile actions was signed in Tehran in September 2004. What happened still? Was there any positive improvement of the political situation in the contiguous state? Perhaps, drug smuggling reduced somehow, or transgressions of frontier lessened? Or maybe a sort of agreement on establishment of some especial friendly relations was reached?

Certainly, the American blitzkrieg in Afghanistan followed by the rapid disappearance of Taliban put the states that were the members of Collective

Security Organization into a meticulous plight having undertaken measures on the strengthening of the mentioned organization which turned to be non-demanded in the course of striking events. Hence a natural desire of the independent Republic of Tajikistan to have a friendly neighbor presented by Afghanistan. Still historically it happened so that in some remote times the unified ethnic community of Tajiks which existed until the state of Manghit dynasty (1753-1920) found itself disjoined.

Tajikistan is not only in want of cooperation, it aspires to it as well. In March 1992, five months before having gained independence, the Ministers of Foreign Affairs from Persian-speaking countries—Islamic Republic of Iran, Republic of Tajikistan and Interim Authority of Afghanistan signed the agreement on cooperation with mujahideen in Tehran. In July 27, 1992, after the power in Afghanistan being assumed by mujahideen, the delegation of ISA which had arrived in Dushanbe for negotiations with the government of Tajikistan discussed a number of programs dwelling on formation of customs station in Ishkashim, construction of a bridge over Pyandzh, development of borderline trade, accomplishment of Faizabad, provincial center of Afghan Badakhshan; Tajikistan being supposed to assist in all the initiations.

As we know, interethnic conflicts inside Afghanistan, including Tajiks and Pashtuns, have deep roots. But the formation of Tajik national self-consciousness went on under complicated historic circumstances, it sustained the sway of neighboring states, Pan-Turkism, regionalism and of other factors and that differs it radically from the national self-consciousness and mentality of the population of Afghanistan. Consolidation of the population of today's Tajik republic as Tajiks crystallized in the Soviet power period being especially stable.

Islamic connection between the neighboring countries is vividly evinced with a part of the population of Tajikistan, especially with Qarotegin group of districts of Gorno-Badakhshan Autonomous region. Upon the whole the analysis of the situation in Tajikistan doesn't deliver convincing examples as to the religious sphere being affected on the part of Afghanistan.

What are the aims pursued by Russia which has created its own military base on the territory of Tajikistan?

Taking into consideration NATO expansion in the direction of the East, the play of Georgia and Azerbaijan with their orientation on the Atlantic bloc, withdrawal of Russian frontier guard troops from Tajikistan, we can say that for the near future the important goal of Russian strategy is a reinstatement of Russian influence upon CIS republics, including Tajikistan. Quoting the analyst of the German newspaper "Die Welt" "its (Russia's) goal is not targeted at restoration of the Soviet Union. Rendering economic support Putin will be insisting on political allegiance in exchange. The criteria of allegiance, perhaps, will be rather simple: participation in the security system being in the competence of Russia and exclusion of extraordinary influence on the part of the third countries (USA, EU, China, Turkey) exercised over CIS countries".

But have all the dangers really vanished and nothing more threatens the security of Tajikistan, other regional countries and those of CIS?

Those Russian frontier guards who were remaining up to July 2005 on the borderlines of Tajikistan and Afghanistan saved not only Tajiks, but themselves either, because the arc of Islamic fundamentalism pierced CIS space. If the frontier is not protected the zone of instability will stop to be Far abroad for Russia.

In combination with the events in the North Caucasus, Chechnya, exodus of Russia from Tajikistan might have complicated the situation not only in Central Asia, but in Russia itself.

Why is the withdrawal of Russian frontier guards from Tajikistan profitable for the USA? Quoting the well-known American politician Zbignev Bzhezinsky, "Central Asia is a strategic crossroad"; and another political scientist named McKinder added that "it is an underpaunch of Hartland". Here the USA probably pursue several strategic goals; they want to participate in tapping of regional natural resources. Taking into account the profitable strategic plight of Tajikistan they do their best to intensify their currency circulation, stock investments into a launch of consortium and various projects.

There was a non-official version running to the effect that in case of introduction of foreign passports for migrants since January 1, 2005 in Russia the latter would be forced to return home and the USA would be prompt to allocate 6 billion dollars for creating job vacancies in Tajikistan, repayment of debts, financing of programs for the formation of trans-frontier passages to uplift Tajikistan from the cul-de-sac isolation, including enhancement of borders. Already today they have got down to a partial equipping of the Tajik-Afghan frontier; for this purpose they meted out communication media, generators, fuel tanks, trucks, uniform and other technique to the total amount of 100 million dollars.

According to official data for 2003 the USA invested approximately 52 % out of the total volume of all entered investments in Tajikistan. Therefore, currently, the more real danger for Russia on the part of NATO is no military one, but it is an economic expansion of Western capital that threatens the country. It is not fortuitous that in the course of his last visit to Tajikistan V.V. Putin undertook a grave step forwarded to intensification of Russian-Tajik cooperation, especially in the branch of economy. In the nearest years Russia intends to invest over 2,3 billion US dollars into the national economy of the republic.

The danger of international extremism and terrorism still remains non-removed.

The USA compose Tajik leadership saying that in case of Russian exodus they will have never left Tajiks in the threatening surroundings of potential penetration of extremists and terrorists from Afghanistan; the American presence being justified by the struggle with those terrorists.

Gradually the European Union has also been starting to join the main donors fortifying the Tajik-Afghan frontier. The program on frontiers management in Central Asia is being effectuated under US aegis; 3,9 million Euros being bound to be disbursed for it in 2005. Only in the first six months of 2005 Brussels allocated 1,65 million Euros for rendering technical assistance to the Committee for state frontier guard in Tajikistan. Additional 1,5 million Euros were promised by the Great Britain. And it is not fortuitous. Drugs production and trafficking in Afghanistan and Big Central Asia is an inevitable reaction to world demands, especially in Europe. So, a solution of this problem for a somehow durable period requires that the demands for drug stuffs in Europe were reduced.

Both moral and practical considerations dictate at least an activation of the role of European Union in supporting the programs on combat with drugs in Big Central Asia and driving this participation up to the level comparable with the multibillion support of analogical programs in Columbia by Washington.

It is clearly seen that today all the states without any exception are alarmed with drug production and trafficking through the frontier of Afghanistan. After the collapse of the USSR the unified frontier guard system disintegrated, now the newly-born states guard their frontiers themselves but it is a new matter for them which is not done up to the mark yet. This situation promoted to the rise of a new route for illegal traffic of drugs across the territories of the former Soviet Union. The mostly intensive conveyance of drugs was carried out since early 1990s in the directions of Khorog-Murgab-Osh, across the Pyandzh, on the western plot of the Tajik-Afghan frontier; another route stretched through Kalai-Khumb to Gharm group of districts. To the beginning to 2000 Shurabad, Moskovsky, Pyandzh and Shaartuz districts became principle directions.

What is the attitude of foreign states and international community to withdrawal of Russian frontier guards from Tajikistan?

The chief of UNO Office for combat with drugs and crimes Antonio Mario Costa after visiting Afghanistan in summer 2004 noted that 80 thousand hectares of land in this country were laid down under opium seeds and 90 per cent of the sprouted product reached Europe. In the period of relative neutralization of Taliban and up to the present moment the production of drugs increased 20 times. Having convinced in dreadful scales of drugs production and its export he stated that one shouldn't haste with the withdrawal of Russian frontier guards.

The assistant of the political science Professor from Yale University P. Luong wrote on this occasion the following: "The United States attained to a considerable extent a limitation of Russian presence in this region. But having done it (the American researcher stresses) they unwittingly opened the doors for other, potentially less desirable regional participants, such as Taliban, Saudi

Arabia, Iran and China. Meanwhile Russia serves as a bridge from Central Asia to the West, i.e. to western values, the above-mentioned Asian States perform the functions of the bridge leading to the South and the East where ruling regimes are less open for western values".

Among European states, perhaps, only France having an airbase in Tajikistan for waging anti-terrorist operations in ISA displays relative indifference to the withdrawal of Russian frontier guards. France considers that their presence is a counteraction against American dominance here; the situation being just the same as on the European continent.

The position of other European states corresponds to their membership in NATO. For example, Germany is inclined in the positive to the withdrawal of Russian frontier guards from Tajikistan as NATO member and an ardent adherent of NATO expansion towards the East. The German position is accounted for by the consideration that the withdrawal of frontier guards provides conditions for realization of the agreement between NATO and Tajikistan government signed in October 2003 when NATO Secretary General George Robertson arrived here; the agreement dwelling on establishment of educational center for frontier guards.

The withdrawal of Russian frontier guard troops from Tajikistan will have naturally satisfied such states as China, Turkey and Pakistan, since the activities of these countries on the territory of Tajikistan are deploying successfully and widely. They deposit their investments, participate in realization of joint projects, take up shares of privatized enterprises, monopolize many branches of economy, strive for applying their educational standards, inspire with their vision of the world, democracy models, cultures putting all it down to the alleged globalization encompassing the planet.

Currently, the frontier plot between the People's Republic of China and the Republic of Tajikistan after the exodus of Russian frontier guards is more under the eye of Chinese than Tajiks, as at the expense of the acquired territorial part of Tajikistan the formers advanced forward. Transport infrastructure is being established. China as an advancing forceful center of today's multi-polar world has been striving to fill the markets of Tajikistan with its cheap goods of respective quality.

Turkey being one of ambitious states which nursed the idea of Great Turan foundation naturally stands for withdrawal of Russian frontier guards from Tajikistan. Turkey's penetration is carried into effect not only from the economic point of view, but mostly in inclusion of a big quantum of their educational establishments—lyceums, Turkish cultural centers ("Shalola"). Multiple times Turkey was promulgating its desire to consolidate and unite all Moslem countries of the region, as being a poly-religious secular state it is inhabited by predominating Moslem population. And, of course, the ideology of Pan-Turkism can be easier exported to the country without frontier guards.

Pakistan having taken a decision to break relations with Taliban and joined the anti-terrorist operation derived maximal benefit, it ensured favorable commercial and economical conditions, foreign aid; now it is exercising great efforts to improve unfriendly relations with the countries which stood against the Taliban regime in former years.

The state which in the recent past supported active members of Hizb-ut-Tahrir and opposing forces of Tajikistan through its Embassy in Dushanbe today tries to invest resources into the construction of Roghun, Sangtuda and other power stations.

The wish to establish lucrative economy ties with secular states of Central Asia, including Tajikistan, against the background of the crushed radical fundamentalism in Afghanistan and the menacing local extremism forced Pakistan to restrict the religious fundamentalism of "their own" in being exported. And it goes without saying that for Pakistan Russian frontier guards would be a hamper as it reckons for Kulob-khorog-Kulma highway to be joined to the transcontinental trunk-roads of Karakarum highway leading in the direction of Karachi after what it might master broadly the market of Tajikistan where their national products might be traded off. The experience of illegal trade through the transparent Afghan-Pakistani frontier can as never be handy in this region.

Withdrawal of Russian frontier guards from Tajikistan may promote to consolidation of partnership relations between Russia and Uzbekistan as the latter will apprehend of active Islamization in the contiguous state and potential penetration of militant groups of the Islamic movement of Uzbekistan and Uzbek Jihad into the Fergana Valley due to the Tajik-Afghan frontier being weakened. By the way, Uzbekistan has stopped clearing of mines their territorial strip adjacent with the Uzbek-Tajik frontier.

So, what consequences may follow the withdrawal of Russian frontier guards from Tajikistan?

Over 3500 Tajik young men served in Russian frontier guard troops as officers, ensigns and mostly as rank and file soldiers. Being transferred into national currency soldier's monthly salary made up 150 somoni while a minimal wage in the republic is 20 somoni. As for officer's salary it was quite fair. In a word, the national treasury was replenished at the expense of money turnover of Russian ruble. The integrated incomes of Tajik military servicemen included into the structure of Russian frontier guards were a significant contribution supporting a certain part of the population. After the exodus of Russians the former military frontier guards seem to be sustaining hardships concerned with subsistence level. Considerable number of civilians was engaged in trade and consumer services sector catering for their needs of frontier guards.

It is calculated that about 50 million dollars are required to maintain the frontier of Tajikistan. And, as it was mentioned, some new partners promise to allocate financial aid for these aims. But the problem lies not only in funds.

Combat training and especially physical training of Tajik frontier guards needs to be much improved. In order to resolve these problems time and financial resources will be in great need.

After the withdrawal of Russian frontier guards, against the background of continuing poor financial support on the part of the state and the augmenting support by Aga Khan the ties of Gorno-Badakhshan Autonomous Region (GBAR) with the Central government may be slackened due to adjusted frontier trade with China, Afghanistan, Kyrgyzstan. Already today taking into account the difficulties of transport communication, especially in an autumnal-winter period, GBAR gives preference to the trade with Osh town, because it brings economic profit. A designed plan of a future motorway is a stretch of 60 km across Vakhan isthmus will enable to shape an internal bordering market. Moreover, foreign investors (Pakistan, PRC, IRI and others) will eagerly deposit money into the lucrative branch of jewelry processing and other spheres of the autonomous region which attracts many businessmen mostly by its strategic fuel resources.

The Government of Tajikistan undertakes consistent principal measures on combat with drug-related crime. These are: foundation of the Committee for combat with illegal circulation of drugs being the first one in the post-Soviet space; consolidation of the leadership of the state committee of frontier guard service; irreconcilable struggle with corruption in state structures declared by the President of the country E.Sh. Rahmonov, and lots of other things.

At the same time one can consider that temporal weakening of the frontier after the withdrawal of Russian military servicemen is tantamount to its enhancing transparence. Transmission of the frontier from Russians to its native owners may be profitable for drug criminals who would like to regulate drug trafficking without being hampered. In some analysts' opinion, the events in Andijan are not at all a "colored revolution" carried into effect in accordance with the designs of West, but an endeavor of criminal elements and middle Asian barons closely cooperating with radical Islamic circles to provide a direct transit channel for conveyance of drugs from Afghanistan to Europe [3].

Sometimes they say that Russian frontier guards also took to this behoof allegedly professing the principle—"when you see a fire you can't help warming yourself". The entire present structure of frontiers' immunity does not compose an integral system. A separate frontier guard irrespective of his nationality doesn't perceive it as a whole organism: if he wants to receive a bribe he merely side-steps the system just assigned for ensuring his own safety. Local residents say you can cross the frontier for 50 dollars. For drug criminals it is a trifling sum. Under such a wide-scale drug diversion this narrow circle of people might be quite probably privy to it.

And now you can easily imagine what would occur from time to time after the frontier is transmitted into the competence of Tajik colleagues: linguistic, cultural, ethnic relations with low living standard of population from both sides may convert the frontier into a passage for drug trafficking abuses.

Today notwithstanding a relatively good protection of the frontier drug couriers not only contrive to find new channels for drug conveyance, but they conduct thorough trainings on simultaneous concordance of actions carried out by several groups at a running. They try to misinform and divert frontier guard forces in order the latter wasted resources in vain, they organize permanent observance over frontier guard activities. They are mobile being perfectly equipped; they use modern media of communications, apparatus of noctovision, radio stations and etc.

Certainly, the young independent Republic of Tajikistan has really got a great deal of problems, including those concerned with the frontier. Here, just as in the whole region of Central Asia, by the way, there focused strategic interests of multiple states. Pursuing the line of pragmatism in foreign policy Tajikistan will be cooperating with all world community when solving its problems.

The aid and specific actions on the part of world community can become a guarantee for effective struggle against international terrorism, illegal circulation of drugs and security in reference to the sovereign Republic of Tajikistan.

Notes:

1. Broadcast "The Voice of Afghanistan" transmitted in August 21, 1991
2. Principal Streamlines of Foreign Policy of the Republic of Uzbekistan. Tashkent. "Uzbekistan"-p.32
3. Middle Asia: Andijan Scenario? M. "Europe" publishing house—p.90
4. Stanislav Chernyavsky. Central Asia in the Epoch of Changes. p.1
5. Frederic Francis. Deficiency of Attention? p. 1-16

CONCLUSION

Geopolitical atmosphere in Central Asia, alongside with such big neighbors as Russia, China, Iran and Turkey will be exercising a direct influence over this region Afghanistan in no case will step aside. Just here, being backed with Pakistan the Islamic extremist organizations concentrated their activities, namely here they produce drug stuffs exported through Central Asian republics to Europe.

The analysis of the civil war in Tajikistan shows that the conflict between the disciples of a national and of a pro-communist state was being complicated under the direct influence of Afghanistan; after the relative weakening in regard to the Tajik-Afghan frontier guarding their intensified a religious sway on the part of the largest religious centers, fundamentalist parties, Al-Qaida movement; the export of drugs and weapons being enhanced.

Historic, cultural and good-neighborly relations between our countries serve as a basis for political and economic ties. The government of Tajikistan undertakes comprehensive measures promoting to reestablishment of peace and stability in Afghanistan, practical support of the lawful government of this country.

The commenced construction of several bridges over the Pyandzh between Tajikistan and Afghanistan, building of trunk-roads roads connecting the southern areas of Tajikistan with Iran through Gerat, power supply by means of stretched PTLs, granting opportunities for Afghan immigrants in studying and mastering various specialties, giving shelters to thousands of Afghan refugees are concrete streamlines of multilateral cooperation between the two states. The building of Kulob-Khorog-Kulma trunk-road when connected to Karakorum highway will enable Tajikistan and the whole Central Asia with its rich fuel-energy resources to create trade border zones between the neighboring countries.

The revival of the Great Silk Road will be conducing to achieve inclusion of Tajikistan and Afghanistan into international labor division.

It is clear that implementation of all these grandiose projects depends on inner political situation in Afghanistan located in the epicenter of Asia.

After the end of the cold war the West presented by the USA assumed the role of international peace-maker. For a certain period of time Afghanistan situated in the center of Asia was forsaken by the USA, European states and world community.

After the downfall of Najibullah, the President of the Democratic Republic of Afghanistan, the power in the country was assumed by mujahideen supported morally and materially by the USA. Regular war drives having taken place in the country annihilated moral and material grounds, manners and orders. There started an unprecedented plunder of all and everything in the country. Law enforcement bodies and national security agencies were paralyzed in accordance with directives from outside.

In 1996 Afghanistan was embraced with darkness. The Taliban movement assumed power being buttressed by Al-Qaida from behind. In the course of four years they brought a lot of harm ruling over 90 per cent of the territory of Afghanistan; not only Moslems suffered from them but representatives of others religions either. The annihilation of unique Buddha statues in Bamyan testifies to their obscurantism. The western world being in remote space was observing over what occurred in the ruined and destroyed Afghanistan enjoying its own safety. But in September 11, 2001 the winds of dark forces blew away the two skyscrapers in Manhattan.

This forwarded to the West dark force whose roots are traced back to Al-Qaida, Taliban and other Islamic forces of fundamentalism, governed by Pakistani OSI and reared owing to the USA support turned against its founders. World community alarmed with the situation in Afghanistan convened Bonn Summit, formed the Interim Coalitional Authority headed by Hamid Karzai and arrived in Kabul.

World community turned its face to Afghanistan offering moral and material humanitarian aid. The USA and European Union declared this country to be a zone of their vitally important interests. They convened the historic Loya Jirga which elected an Interim Coalitional Authority. The second Loya Jirga adopted the Constitution of Afghanistan which paved the way to general elections of the country's President.

The President was elected on an alternative democratic basis. It was Hamid Karzai. Later on being supported by world community they elected a two-chamber Parliament (upper and low): Wolesi Jirga (lower house) and Meshrano Jirga (upper house). The Parliament reviewed and approved the staff of the government proposed by the President.

Presently, the security agencies and law e`nforcement bodies established with the assistance of world community began an organized struggle against terrorism and drug-related crime. The society realized that without eradication of these dangers it will be impossible to dwell on stabilization of political situation in the country. Pursuing these goals world community started rendering of universal financial and moral aid in training and educating of human resources predestined to solve the problems of combat with the menaces pointed. In the South and the North of the country many officers of security agencies and law enforcement bodies had fallen victims to the fight with terrorists. Nevertheless, only they are able to bring impediments on the way of various forms of crimes—drug trafficking and weapon delivery to the neighboring Central Asian states, kidnapping of children and adults as hostages on their territories, subversive actions performed by shahids-kamikazes, religious extremism.

In spite of grave progresses on the world community part made in the cause of returning relative peace and stability to Afghanistan this country has been colliding with serious problems up to now. Due to peculiar geographic and historic location Afghanistan was isolated from political and social events of the contemporary world being far from it.

Today Afghanistan has been faced with the next challenges and problems:

- urgency in full ensuring of security;
- enforcement of combat with drug addiction;
- establishment of national army and police, as well as legal regime of Afghanistan;
- liquidation of non-subordination of some local authorities to the central state and non-admittance of inappropriate interference of some foreign countries in internal affairs of Afghanistan.

It is important to take into account that if commitments of world community on rendering aid to Afghanistan are not effected and necessary economic and financial investments are not implemented there will not be any guarantee from Afghanistan that it wouldn't have retuned to the bitter times of civil war and crisis.

The Republic of Tajikistan has been consistently pursuing the policy aimed at establishment of a strong, stable and free neighboring state with developing economy being always ready to promote to achievement of this noble goal.

Now Afghanistan finds itself at a crucial turning-point: from confrontation to concordance and creative labor.

2724175R00054

Printed in Great Britain
by Amazon.co.uk, Ltd.,
Marston Gate.